The Essential E

JAGUAR/DAIMLER
XJ40

Your marque expert:
Peter Crespin

VELOCE PUBLISHING
THE PUBLISHER OF FINE AUTOMOTIVE BOOKS

Other great books from Veloce –

Speedpro Series
4-cylinder Engine – How To Blueprint & Build A Short Block For High Performance (Hammill)
Alfa Romeo DOHC High-performance Manual (Kartalamakis)
Alfa Romeo V6 Engine High-performance Manual (Kartalamakis)
BMC 998cc A-series Engine – How To Power Tune (Hammill)
1275cc A-series High-performance Manual (Hammill)
Camshafts – How To Choose & Time Them For Maximum Power (Hammill)
Competition Car Datalogging Manual, The (Templeman)
Cylinder Heads – How To Build, Modify & Power Tune Updated & Revised Edition (Burgess & Gollan)
Distributor-type Ignition Systems – How To Build & Power Tune (Hammill)
Fast Road Car – How To Plan And Build Revised & Updated Colour New Edition (Stapleton)
Ford SOHC 'Pinto' & Sierra Cosworth DOHC Engines – How To Power Tune Updated & Enlarged Edition (Hammill)
Ford V8 – How To Power Tune Small Block Engines (Hammill)
Harley-Davidson Evolution Engines – How To Build & Power Tune (Hammill)
Holley Carburetors – How To Build & Power Tune Revised & Updated Edition (Hammill)
Jaguar XK Engines – How To Power Tune Revised & Updated Colour Edition (Hammill)
MG Midget & Austin-Healey Sprite – How To Power Tune Updated & Enlarged 3rd Edition (Stapleton)
MGB 4-cylinder Engine – How To Power Tune (Burgess)
MGB V8 Power – How To Give Your, Third Colour Edition (Williams)
MGB, MGC & MGB V8 – How To Improve New 2nd Edition (Williams)
Mini Engines – How To Power Tune On A Small Budget Colour Edition (Hammill)
Motorcycle-engined Racing Car – How To Build (Pashley)
Motorsport – Getting Started in (Collins)
Nitrous Oxide High-performance Manual, The (Langfield)
Rover V8 Engines – How To Power Tune (Hammill)
Sportscar/kitcar Suspension & Brakes – How To Build & Modify Revised 3rd Edition (Hammill)
SU Carburettor High-performance Manual (Hammill)
Suzuki 4x4 – How To Modify For Serious Off-road Action (Richardson)
Tiger Avon Sportscar – How To Build Your Own Updated & Revised 2nd Edition (Dudley)
TR2, 3 & TR4 – How To Improve (Williams)
TR5, 250 & TR6 – How To Improve (Williams)
TR7 & TR8 – How To Improve (Williams)
V8 Engine – How To Build A Short Block For High Performance (Hammill)
Volkswagen Beetle Suspension, Brakes & Chassis – How To Modify For High Performance (Hale)
Volkswagen Bus Suspension, Brakes & Chassis – How To Modify For High Performance (Hale)
Weber DCOE, & Dellorto DHLA Carburetors – How To Build & Power Tune 3rd Edition (Hammill)

Those Were The Days ... Series
Alpine Trials & Rallies 1910-1973 (Pfundner)
Austerity Motoring (Bobbitt)
Brighton National Speed Trials (Gardiner)
British Police Cars (Walker)
British Woodies (Peck)
Dune Buggy Phenomenon (Hale)
Dune Buggy Phenomenon Volume 2 (Hale)
Hot Rod & Stock Car Racing in Britain In The 1980s (Neil)
MG's Abingdon Factory (Moylan)
Motor Racing At Brands Hatch In The Seventies (Parker)
Motor Racing At Crystal Palace (Collins)
Motor Racing At Goodwood In The Sixties (Gardiner)
Motor Racing At Nassau In The 1950s & 1960s (O'Neil)
Motor Racing At Oulton Park In The 1960s (Mcfadyen)
Motor Racing At Oulton Park In The 1970s (Mcfadyen)
Three Wheelers (Bobbitt)

Enthusiast's Restoration Manual Series
Citroën 2CV, How To Restore (Porter)
Classic Car Bodywork, How To Restore (Thaddeus)
Classic Car Electrics (Thaddeus)
Classic Cars, How To Paint (Thaddeus)
Reliant Regal, How To Restore (Payne)
Triumph TR2/3/3A, How To Restore (Williams)
Triumph TR4/4A, How To Restore (Williams)
Triumph TR5/250 & 6, How To Restore (Williams)
Triumph TR7/8, How To Restore (Williams)
Volkswagen Beetle, How To Restore (Tyler)
VW Bay Window Bus (Paxton)
Yamaha FS1-E, How To Restore (Watts)

Essential Buyer's Guide Series
Alfa GT (Booker)
Alfa Romeo Spider Giulia (Booker & Talbott)
BMW GS (Henshaw)
BSA Bantam (Henshaw)
BSA Twins (Henshaw)
Citroën 2CV (Paxton)
Citroën ID & DS (Heilig)
Fiat 500 & 600 (Bobbitt)
Jaguar E-type 3.8 & 4.2-litre (Crespin)
Jaguar E-type V12 5.3-litre (Crespin)
Jaguar/Daimler XJ6, XJ12 & Sovereign (Crespin)
Jaguar XJ-S (Crespin)
MGB & MGB GT (Williams)
Mercedes-Benz 280SL-560DSL Roadsters (Bass)
Mercedes-Benz 'Pagoda' 230SL, 250SL & 280SL Roadsters & Coupés (Bass)
Morris Minor & 1000 (Newell)
Porsche 928 (Hemmings)
Rolls-Royce Silver Shadow & Bentley T-Series (Bobbitt)
Subaru Impreza (Hobbs)
Triumph Bonneville (Henshaw)
Triumph TR6 (Williams)
VW Beetle (Cservenka & Copping)
VW Bus (Cservenka & Copping)

Auto-Graphics Series
Fiat-based Abarths (Sparrow)
Jaguar MKI & II Saloons (Sparrow)
Lambretta Li Series Scooters (Sparrow)

Rally Giants Series
Audi Quattro (Robson)
Austin Healey 100-6 & 3000 (Robson)
Fiat 131 Abarth (Robson)
Ford Escort MkI (Robson)
Ford Escort RS Cosworth & World Rally Car (Robson)
Ford Escort RS1800 (Robson)
Lancia Stratos (Robson)
Peugeot 205 T16 (Robson)
Subaru Impreza (Robson)

General
1½-litre GP Racing 1961-1965 (Whitelock)
AC Two-litre Saloons & Buckland Sportscars (Archibald)
Alfa Romeo Giulia Coupé GT & GTA (Tipler)
Alfa Romeo Montreal – The Essential Companion (Taylor)
Alfa Tipo 33 (McDonough & Collins)
Alpine & Renault – The Development Of The Revolutionary Turbo F1 Car 1968 to 1979 (Smith)
Anatomy Of The Works Minis (Moylan)
Armstrong-Siddeley (Smith)
Autodrome (Collins & Ireland)
Automotive A-Z, Lane's Dictionary Of Automotive Terms (Lane)
Automotive Mascots (Kay & Springate)
Bahamas Speed Weeks, The (O'Neil)
Bentley Continental, Corniche And Azure (Bennett)
Bentley MkVI, Rolls-Royce Silver Wraith, Dawn & Cloud/Bentley R & S-Series (Nutland)
BMC Competitions Department Secrets (Turner, Chambers Browning)
BMW 5-Series (Cranswick)
BMW Z-Cars (Taylor)
Britains Farm Model Balers & Combines 1967 to 2007 (Pullen)
British 250cc Racing Motorcycles (Pereira)
British Cars, The Complete Catalogue Of, 1895-1975 (Culshaw & Horrobin)
BRM – A Mechanic's Tale (Salmon)
BRM V16 (Ludvigsen)
BSA Bantam Bible, The (Henshaw)
Bugatti Type 40 (Price)
Bugatti 46/50 Updated Edition (Price & Arbey)
Bugatti T44 & T49 (Price & Arbey)
Bugatti 57 2nd Edition (Price)
Caravans, The Illustrated History 1919-1959 (Jenkinson)
Caravans, The Illustrated History From 1960 (Jenkinson)
Carrera Panamericana, La (Tipler)
Chrysler 300 – America's Most Powerful Car 2nd Edition (Ackerson)
Chrysler PT Cruiser (Ackerson)
Citroën DS (Bobbitt)
Cliff Allison – From The Fells To Ferrari (Gauld)
Cobra – The Real Thing! (Legate)
Cortina – Ford's Bestseller (Robson)
Coventry Climax Racing Engines (Hammill)
Daimler SP250 New Edition (Long)
Datsun Fairlady Roadster To 280ZX – The Z-Car Story (Long)
Dino – The V6 Ferrari (Long)
Dodge Charger – Enduring Thunder (Ackerson)
Dodge Dynamite! (Grist)
Donington (Boddy)
Draw & Paint Cars – How To (Gardiner)
Drive On The Wild Side, A – 20 Extreme Driving Adventures From Around The World (Weaver)
Ducati 750 Bible, The (Falloon)
Ducati 860, 900 And Mille Bible, The (Falloon)
Dune Buggy, Building A – The Essential Manual (Shakespeare)
Dune Buggy Files (Hale)
Dune Buggy Handbook (Hale)
Edward Turner: The Man Behind The Motorcycles (Clew)
Fiat & Abarth 124 Spider & Coupé (Tipler)
Fiat & Abarth 500 & 600 2nd Edition (Bobbitt)
Fiats, Great Small (Ward)
Fine Art Of The Motorcycle Engine, The (Peirce)
Ford F100/F150 Pick-up 1948-1996 (Ackerson)
Ford F150 Pick-up 1997-2005 (Ackerson)
Ford GT – Then, And Now (Streather)
Ford GT40 (Legate)
Ford In Miniature (Olson)
Ford Model Y (Roberts)
Ford Thunderbird From 1954, The Book Of The (Long)
Forza Minardi! (Vigar)
Funky Mopeds (Skelton)
Gentleman Jack (Gauld)
GM In Miniature (Olson)
GT – The World's Best GT Cars 1953-73 (Dawson)
Hillclimbing & Sprinting – The Essential Manual (Short & Wilkinson)
Honda NSX (Long)
Jaguar, The Rise Of (Price)
Jaguar XJ-S (Long)
Jeep CJ (Ackerson)
Jeep Wrangler (Ackerson)
Karmann-Ghia Coupé & Convertible (Bobbitt)
Lamborghini Miura Bible, The (Sackey)
Lambretta Bible, The (Davies)
Lancia 037 (Collins)
Lancia Delta HF Integrale (Blaettel & Wagner)
Land Rover, The Half-ton Military (Cook)
Laverda Twins & Triples Bible 1968-1986 (Falloon)
Lea-Francis Story, The (Price)
Lexus Story, The (Long)
little book of smart, the (Jackson)
Lola – The Illustrated History (1957-1977) (Starkey)
Lola – All The Sports Racing & Single-seater Racing Cars 1978-1997 (Starkey)
Lola T70 – The Racing History & Individual Chassis Record 4th Edition (Starkey)
Lotus 49 (Oliver)
Marketingmobiles, The Wonderful Wacky World Of (Hale)
Mazda MX-5/Miata 1.6 Enthusiast's Workshop Manual (Grainger & Shoemark)
Mazda MX-5/Miata 1.8 Enthusiast's Workshop Manual (Grainger & Shoemark)
Mazda MX-5 Miata: The Book Of The World's Favourite Sportscar (Long)
Mazda MX-5 Miata Roadster (Long)
MGA (Price Williams)
MGB & MGB GT– Expert Guide (Auto-doc Series) (Williams)
MGB Electrical Systems (Astley)
Micro Caravans (Jenkinson)
Micro Trucks (Mort)
Microcars At Large! (Quellin)
Mini Cooper – The Real Thing! (Tipler)
Mitsubishi Lancer Evo, The Road Car & WRC Story (Long)
Montlhéry, The Story Of The Paris Autodrome (Boddy)
Morgan Maverick (Lawrence)
Morris Minor, 60 Years On The Road (Newell)
Moto Guzzi Sport & Le Mans Bible (Falloon)
Motor Movies – The Posters! (Veysey)
Motor Racing – Reflections Of A Lost Era (Carter)
Motorcycle Apprentice (Cakebread)
Motorcycle Road & Racing Chassis Designs (Noakes)
Motorhomes, The Illustrated History (Jenkinson)
Motorsport In colour, 1950s (Wainwright)
Nissan 300ZX & 350Z – The Z-Car Story (Long)
Off-Road Giants! – Heroes of 1960s Motorcycle Sport (Westlake)
Pass The Theory And Practical Driving Tests (Gibson & Hoole)
Peking To Paris 2007 (Young)
Plastic Toy Cars Of The 1950s & 1960s (Ralston)
Pontiac Firebird (Cranswick)
Porsche Boxster (Long)
Porsche 964, 993 & 996 Data Plate Code Breaker (Streather)
Porsche 356 (2nd Edition) (Long)
Porsche 911 Carrera – The Last Of The Evolution (Corlett)
Porsche 911R, RS & RSR, 4th Edition (Starkey)
Porsche 911 – The Definitive History 1963-1971 (Long)
Porsche 911 – The Definitive History 1971-1977 (Long)
Porsche 911 – The Definitive History 1977-1987 (Long)
Porsche 911 – The Definitive History 1987-1997 (Long)
Porsche 911 – The Definitive History 1997-2004 (Long)
Porsche 911SC 'Super Carrera' – The Essential Companion (Streather)
Porsche 914 & 914-6: The Definitive History Of The Road & Competition Cars (Long)
Porsche 924 (Long)
Porsche 944 (Long)
Porsche 993 'King Of Porsche' – The Essential Companion (Streather)
Porsche 996 'Supreme Porsche' – The Essential Companion (Streather)
Porsche Racing Cars – 1953 To 1975 (Long)
Porsche Racing Cars – 1976 On (Long)
Porsche – The Rally Story (Meredith)
Porsche: Three Generations Of Genius (Meredith)
RAC Rally Action! (Gardiner)
Rallye Sport Fords: The Inside Story (Moreton)
Redman, Jim – 6 Times World Motorcycle Champion: The Autobiography (Redman)
Rolls-Royce Silver Shadow/Bentley T Series Corniche & Camargue Revised & Enlarged Edition (Bobbitt)
Rolls-Royce Silver Spirit, Silver Spur & Bentley Mulsanne 2nd Edition (Bobbitt)
RX-7 – Mazda's Rotary Engine Sportscar (Updated & Revised New Edition) (Long)
Scooters & Microcars, The A-Z Of Popular (Dan)
Scooter Lifestyle (Grainger)
Singer Story: Cars, Commercial Vehicles, Bicycles & Motorcycle (Atkinson)
SM – Citroën's Maserati-engined Supercar (Long & Claverol)
Subaru Impreza: The Road Car And WRC Story (Long)
Supercar, How To Build your own (Thompson)
Taxi! The Story Of The 'London' Taxicab (Bobbitt)
Tinplate Toy Cars Of The 1950s & 1960s (Ralston)
Toyota Celica & Supra, The Book Of Toyota's Sports Coupés (Long)
Toyota MR2 Coupés & Spyders (Long)
Triumph Motorcycles & The Meriden Factory (Hancox)
Triumph Speed Twin & Thunderbird Bible (Woolridge)
Triumph Tiger Cub Bible (Estall)
Triumph Trophy Bible (Woolridge)
Triumph TR6 (Kimberley)
Unraced (Collins)
Velocette Motorcycles – MSS To Thruxton Updated & Revised (Burris)
Virgil Exner – Visioneer: The Official Biography Of Virgil M Exner Designer Extraordinaire (Grist)
Volkswagen Bus Book, The (Bobbitt)
Volkswagen Bus Or Van To Camper, How To Convert (Porter)
Volkswagens Of The World (Glen)
VW Beetle Cabriolet (Bobbitt)
VW Beetle – The Car Of The 20th Century (Copping)
VW Bus – 40 Years Of Splitties, Bays & Wedges (Copping)
VW Bus Book, The (Bobbitt)
VW Golf: Five Generations Of Fun (Copping & Cservenka)
VW – The Air-cooled Era (Copping)
VW T5 Camper Conversion Manual (Porter)
VW Campers (Copping)
Works Minis, The Last (Purves & Brenchley)
Works Rally Mechanic (Moylan)

www.veloce.co.uk

First published in December 2008 by Veloce Publishing Limited, 33 Trinity Street, Dorchester DT1 1TT, England. Fax 01305 268864/e-mail info@veloce.co.uk/ web www.veloce.co.uk or www.velocebooks.com.
ISBN: 978-1-84584-192-8/UPC: 6-368470-4192-2

© Peter Crespin and Veloce Publishing 2009. All rights reserved. With the exception of quoting brief passages for the purpose of review, no part of this publication may be recorded, reproduced or transmitted by any means, including photocopying, without the written permission of Veloce Publishing Ltd. Throughout this book logos, model names and designations, etc, have been used for the purposes of identification, illustration and decoration. Such names are the property of the trademark holder as this is not an official publication.

Readers with ideas for automotive books, or books on other transport or related hobby subjects, are invited to write to the editorial director of Veloce Publishing at the above address.
British Library Cataloguing in Publication Data - A catalogue record for this book is available from the British Library. Typesetting, design and page make-up all by Veloce Publishing Ltd on Apple Mac. Printed in India by Replika Press.

Introduction & thanks
– the purpose of this book

Introduction

Launched after a 14-year gestation, the XJ40 was the first totally new Jaguar 4-door for 18 years. Production ceased in 1994 but the basic shell continued to 2003 and the final steel-bodied XJ8*. This book is designed to help you decide which, if any, XJ40 model to buy from the 5 engines and wide range of trim levels and models available.

The XJ40 (never badged as such, incidentally) featured technology new to Jaguar in almost all systems, and was certainly the most complex car the company had designed up to then, with a digital dashboard and many electronic systems and computers. Consequently, it underwent Jaguar's most extensive testing programme, from the first driveable prototype in 1981, through tests in Death Valley and Australia, (which my best friend Tim Brooks helped with), to launch in 1986. Thankfully, after some teething troubles, most of the technology came good, and the XJ40 can provide refined and comfortable transport for years, given basic care.

Most XJ40 development was during the British Leyland years, and the car was designed specifically to prevent fitment of the Buick-derived Rover V8 (to prevent Jaguar's own engines being sidelined). Sadly, this meant that the V12 would not fit either, and it wasn't until the final two years of XJ40 production that this situation was remedied with the fabulous 6.0L XJ81 in Jaguar XJ12 and Daimler Double Six versions.

The XJ40 came to fruition during John Egan's quality drive and, although over 5 million miles of testing didn't iron out every bug by launch, it was good enough to show the potential of the small Jaguar company, and attract massive Ford investment. Ford production expertise improved the last 3.2 and 4.0L models greatly and Jaguar took them to the next level with the X300 in 1994*.

Large numbers were sold, many are still around, and they make a great value car provided you buy a good example. This book aims to help you do so by describing the main things to check on any potential purchase. It's small enough to take with you when inspecting a car, and detailed enough to help you avoid buying a bad example. Over 200,000 XJ40s were produced, so there are plenty left. Happy hunting!

Acknowledgements

I owe much to the XJ40 owners whose cooperation and help with photographs and information have been invaluable, in particular Bryan Neish, Mike Stevens, Gregory Scotlander, Hans Goerlitzer, Naseem Mohammed, Aaron Goldman, Steve Woodward and others.

Peter Crespin
Cambridge

*(See the Veloce 1994-2003 XJ Buyer's Guide)

Contents

Introduction & thanks
– the purpose of this book 3

1 Is it the right car for you?
– marriage guidance 5

2 Cost considerations
– affordable, or a money pit? 8

3 Living with an XJ:
– will you get along together? 11

4 Relative values:
– which model for you? 12

5 Before you view:
– be well informed 14

6 Inspection equipment
– these items will really help 18

7 Fifteen minute evaluation
– walk away or stay? 21

8 Key points
– where to look for problems 25

9 Serious evaluation
– 60 minutes for years of
enjoyment....................................28

10 Auctions
– sold! Another way to buy your
dream..41

11 Paperwork
– correct documentation is
essential! 43

12 What's it worth?
– let your head rule your heart! 45

13 Do you really want to restore?
– it'll take longer and cost more
than you think...............................48

14 Paint problems
– a bad complexion, including
dimples, pimples and bubbles 50

15 Problems due to lack of use
– just like their owners, XJ40s need
exercise..52

16 The Community
– key people, organisations and
companies in the XJ40 world........55

17 Vital statistics
– essential data at your fingertips.....58

Index..64

Essential Buyer's Guide™ currency
At the time of publication a BG unit of currency "●" equals approximately £1.00/
US$2.00/Euro 1.50. Please adjust to suit current exchange rates.

www.velocebooks.com / www.veloce.co.uk
All current books • New book news • Special offers • Gift vouchers

1 Is it the right car for you?
– marriage guidance!

Tall and short drivers
All XJ40s seats are multi-adjustable with lumbar support and electric operation (plus eventually memory function) on higher-spec models. There is lots of driver leg room, although the handbrake can intrude. Steering is either reach or rake adjustable depending on year. Headroom is good, even if a factory electric sunroof is fitted, although it is better without.

Weight of controls
All XJ40s have well-weighted power steering which is heavier on sports models. Most XJ40s (and all American cars) are automatics, but manual cars have a reasonable clutch and good gear change, at a stretch. XJ40s have discs all round which stop the car well, with a progressive pedal pressure. The handbrake is convenient and not heavy to use.

Will it fit the garage?
Length: 4990mm/16ft 4.5in (LWB add 100mm/4in)
Width: 2000mm/6ft 6.5in
Height: 1380mm/54.5in

Interior space
The XJ40 is a comfortable car for five adults, although rear legroom is not huge with the front seats fully back. Daimler/ Vanden Plas models with individual rear seats are designed for two rear passengers, although three can fit. Head and shoulder room is good. Long wheelbase special editions are rare.

Luggage capacity
The XJ40 has a large, deep boot but the spare wheel intrudes slightly, as do the silencer recesses (and the battery on 93/94 models). All doors have generous oddment bins, a box for cassettes, etc,

Room for tall expert Bryan Neish.

Adjustable steering wheels assist driver fit.

Generous glove box and oddment space.

under the armrest and a lockable glove box in the passenger fascia. Some Daimler and Vanden Plas models had an additional cubby in the rear centre armrest. There are also map or magazine pockets behind the front seats.

Running costs

XJ40 fuel consumption increases with engine size and all models are thirsty. The 2.9 models were theoretically the most frugal but have to be worked hard, so the advantage is not great. Being large cars, they need to be driven for good distances to get properly warm and are not suited to exclusively short trips, which affects running costs in an age of spiralling fuel prices. On the other hand, this means some fabulously appointed cars are available cheaply, so initial costs can be very low. For use as daily transport, a conversion to liquefied gas fuel makes sense (in Europe at least, where there is an excellent LPG infrastructure) at the cost of boot space unless you run with a round tank and no spare wheel. Depending on transmission, driving style and gearing, you'll get around 17-20mpg (Imperial) from a 93-94 V12 (technically known as the XJ81), with less in the city

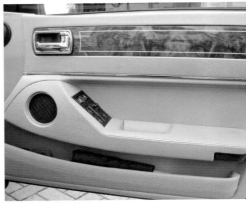

Early-style door pocket.

and potentially slightly more on the open road. The 3.6 can give mid-twenties miles per gallon and the later 3.2 and 4.0L engines a fraction more. The 2.9 can stretch to 30 if driven very gently. Unless driven predominantly in town, service intervals are around 6-7000 miles/6 months, and mostly consist of fluid checks/changes, plus air and fuel filters, plugs every other service and gearbox, differential, brake and coolant fluids every two years. Metric tyres are expensive. Being complex cars, the many rubber suspension parts eventually wear out and, although the anti-roll bar and upper wishbone bushes are not expensive to replace, the lower wishbone and A-frame bushes cost more. Servicing and problem-solving can be DIY but are not quite as basic as the older carburettor cars.

Usability

XJ40s are comfortable, cosseting cars, suited to even the longest trips. Many survivors are still daily transport and, with low purchase prices, the running costs are normally manageable although a smaller, more frugal car is useful back-up if problems arise. Short, infrequent trips are much harder on the car than regular

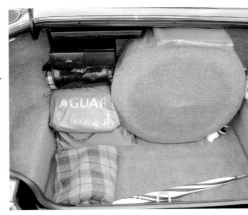

Luggage room: good but not great.

use and long runs where the big engine can warm up fully. All North American cars and most others have air conditioning, which makes their use in hot climates a pleasure.

Parts availability
There are many specialists who can supply almost every part new (many still made by Jaguar) except for some early trim. There are also many dismantled cars from which to supply secondhand components. The AJ6 engine was used in the XJ-S, so many mechanical parts fit both. Some parts carried over to the 94-97 X300 models, especially from the last couple of years of XJ40 production.

Parts cost
Dealer parts are top quality and the price reflects this, but equivalent or near-equivalent quality can be obtained from normal generic parts sources, especially for consumables. Servicing can involve large labour bills for diagnosing elusive faults or fitting certain parts such as front subframe mounts.

Insurance
As large-engined prestige cars, XJ40s are not the cheapest to insure but most qualify for 'classic' insurance if a 15 year rule is applied. Other cheap insurance can be obtained from owner's club or specialist schemes (see Chapter 16). Get several quotes and investigate limited mileage or club policies to keep costs down.

Investment potential
XJ40s are not rare cars and have not yet achieved full 'classic' status, apart from possibly one or two very rare models. They are therefore not investment vehicles in the usual sense. Drive one because you enjoy the ride, not because you want to make money.

Alternatives
By the time the XJ40 arrived, other companies were producing large cars with good ride and handling, though normally at a higher price. Most alternatives would be German or American luxury cars – such as the Mercedes S class, BMW 7 series, Lincolns or Cadillacs, with one or two European makes and the very earliest Lexus cars also being rivals. Rolls-Royce or Bentley alternatives can be found for slightly more money but running costs can be crippling. Italian 12 cylinder exotica were rarely anything but highly-strung GT or sports cars and are very expensive to buy and maintain. A top-end Rover SD1 or top-of-the-range Citroën CX is a viable option but without the class of the Jaguar or Daimler.

Check your garage length.

2 Cost considerations
– affordable, or a money pit?

Purchase price

No XJ40 should be more expensive than the cheapest new micro car on the market, but offer a lot more style and safety. They are probably the cheapest Jaguars of all, and even the best cars are comparatively affordable. However, as the saying goes, "there is nothing more expensive than a cheap Jaguar," so buy the very best you can afford. Those who want a really good

6.0L: not quite as thirsty as the Spitfire V12.

car should look at the top of the market and seek out immaculate examples at specialist independent Jaguar dealers, to have a reliable and durable vehicle from the start. Good dealers are choosy and turn away dozens of XJ40s for every top car accepted for resale.

If you just want to try a Jaguar to see if the bug bites, it is possible to find a good car privately, but this book or a knowledgeable friend will be essential to avoid buying a bad example. There is little point paying for a project car or non-runner, since these are often worth little more than scrap value, and are useful more as a parts car or source of cheap upgrades than a 'fixer-upper.'

Affordable to run?

For XJ40s to be used regularly it is important to include fuel, servicing, consumables and insurance when deciding whether the car will be affordable to run. Modern cars

Great value luxury.

depreciate but have low running costs. XJ40s are generally the opposite and are mostly now at the bottom of their lifetime price range, apart from rare sports or special edition models which may fall further if neglected. If you want a car that will go on for year after year with nothing more than oil, water and fuel then you are underestimating the commitment of owning a large classic that was not cheap to run when new and will not be cheap to run 20-30 years later.

Price bands

If you're looking for an excellent show car you'll need to spend several thousand – maybe ●x 5000 or more. A respectable daily driver with a few minor issues should be available for ●x 2000 or less, depending on market conditions locally. Bargain cars, especially if they have just passed inspection, can be had for ●x 750-1000 but anything much lower should probably be avoided except with a known good service record etc, or if traded between friends or family.

Buy a wreck, build for years

Avoid the alternative strategy for more expensive classic Jaguars – that of paying little for a poor or incomplete car, then buying parts as you build the vehicle yourself or pay a workshop to do so. This approach is normally pointless with an XJ40, as there are so many complete running cars for immediate use and gradual improvement.

Servicing

Job	Interval
Basic oil change	3000 miles
Annual service	6-7000 miles or 12 months
Major service	18,000 miles or 3 yearly
Adjust valve clearances	24,000 miles or 4 yearly
Other?	As needed

Cheapest is rarely best value.

XJ40 Series parts prices*

Mechanical parts
Brake pads (front) ●x 55
Brake pads (rear) ●x 26
Head gasket set ●x 80
Coil ●x 33
Fuel pump ●x 211
Exhaust mid-cats ●x 369
Exhaust front section ●x 60
Radiator ●x 225
Alternator ●x 241

Water pump ●x 195
Shock absorbers (front) ●x 72
Shock absorbers (rear) ●x 59
Starter motor ●x 187
Air con compressor ●x 575
Air con condenser ●x 215
Receiver/dryer ●x 51
Wheel bearings (front) ●x 28
Wheel bearings (rear) ●x 28
Wishbone bushes ●x 13
Thermostat ●x 13

Body and trim parts
Door skin ● x 62
Headlight ● x 111
Windscreen ● x 124
Front wing ● x 111
Bumper beam ● x 111
Bumper cover ● x 172
Rear light cluster ● x 73
Rear light lens n/a
Driver's seat cover/repair n/a
Carpet set n/a
Overmats ● x 62
Headlining material n/a

Used parts
There are many XJ40s being broken for spares privately or by the trade.
Check Classic Vehicle Press
eBay tends to list fewer spare parts for XJ40s than it does for more valuable classics, but you can see which Jaguar dismantlers operate in your market.
Owner's club classifieds
Autojumbles/swapmeets

*Prices exclude UK tax (not payable on export orders).Courtesy SNG Barratt Ltd.

A marque of distinction.

Good points

Roomy luxury car for little money.

Distinctive shape and imposing presence.

Models for most tastes and needs.

Strong engines and transmissions.

Well-equipped with most creature comforts.

Smooth power and performance, with great refinement.

Excellent ride and comfort, without soggy handling.

Good steering and brakes for a big car.

Full instrumentation and lots of extras if required.

Safe and strong vehicle if not excessively corroded.

User-serviceable, especially 6-cylinder cars.

Good spares back-up.

Bad points

Can rust very badly – even late cars.

Fuel consumption, especially large engines and autos.

Headlining and trim often worn or damaged.

Screen can cloud and scratch from single wiper.

Screen surround corrosion front or rear.

Cost of V12 engine work and some specialist parts.

Complex suspension often requires refurbishment.

Long rear overhang when parking.

Reliability of some original electrical connectors and parts.

Cost of metric tyres on some models.

Summary

A great roomy car, blighted by some electrical reliability issues today, as components and connections age. A good one should run long and strong, provided the fuel consumption is manageable. Requires regular maintenance and use to give off its best. Not really worth restoring although refreshing a fair example is worth doing if the price is right.

The V12 XJ81 is a superb and very quick car, which also handles if the sport pack is fitted. All are great mile-eaters – luxurious enough to pamper, sporting enough to thrill. This model got better and better as quality improved and late ones are superb value if you find a good example.

A car for classic road trips.

4 Relative values
– which model for you?

Ian Nisbet's upmarket model.

Models

There are many Series XJ40 models but, apart from the 2.9L cars (not imported to North America), price depends more on condition and specification than model. In most markets there are five engines, three main trim levels (base, Sovereign and Daimler/Vanden Plas) plus Sport and other limited editions to choose from, with manual versions of all cars (except North America) apart from the 6.0L V12 which was auto-only.

The best choice depends on availability and intended use. Someone wanting an XJ40 for gentle driving may manage with a 2.9, but the best value and best pricing value is increasingly found in the Sovereign or higher spec models, the later the better. The 1993-94 cars came with many extras as standard, improvements in several key systems, and are generally the pick of the bunch. The XJ12/Daimler Double Six represented a welcome return to the USA for V12 saloons, which were not officially imported after the first handful of Series 3 XJ cars in 1979.

The early cars are distinctive with their electronic dashboards and uncluttered looks, but good ones are scarce. Generally, the later the car, the better the build quality and the better the fuel consumption, which is reflected in higher asking prices. A few Majestic long wheelbase/high roofline special order models were sold but you are unlikely to come across these. The sporting XJ40s were Jaguar's attempt to create a new younger fan base, which capitalised on the company's renaissance in competition through various Touring Car and Le Mans victories in the 1980s. A good one is a better driver's car than a standard saloon but their appeal is narrower, despite none being remotely 'hardcore' sports cars.

Jaguar did not use the Daimler name in North America in modern times, so the Vanden Plas brand was used for top-of-the-range models, featuring extra bright work, boxwood inlaid veneers and full leather trim instead of a mixture of leather and vinyl.

Rare Insignia special edition.

Values

Due to the many models, engines, trim levels etc, the following are simplified and approximate values only. The dearest models are rated at 100% and others shown as a percentage of that value. Note, however, that the price you pay for a given model should depend more on condition than its notional value in this table. Unlike most other Jaguars, these comparatively modern cars have not really fallen into 'desirable' versus 'less desirable' groups and, therefore, the spread of values is not as pronounced. A good car from a supposed low price group may sell for more than a less clean car from a higher group.

When new, automatic transmission cost extra and manual transmission was the base specification. Today, because of rarity, changing tastes and fuel economy benefits, manuals may command a premium. This applies especially in North America, where manual XJ40s were not imported.

Similarly, Daimler or sports models which originally cost significantly more than normal occasionally sell more slowly today, due to their niche appeal compared to equivalent Jaguars. A good Daimler with all the trimmings is still a fine car, though, and in the USA a VDP will almost always cost more. The issue with some of the less common models is that whilst they may be worth more on paper, it can take longer to a find a buyer who recognises the value and therefore sometimes they sell for no more, or occasionally less, than a mainstream model.

All values will vary according to condition and market.

V12 Daimler Double Six/Jaguar XJ12	**100%**
93/94 4.0L Sovereign	**85%**
4.0L XJR	**85%**
3.6L XJR	**75%**
91-92 4.0L Sovereign	**65%**
86-91 3.6 Daimler/VDP	**60%**
86-90 2.9L Daimler/Sovereign	**45%**
86-90 2.9L XJ6	**35%**

Conversions normally reduce value.

5 Before you view
– be well informed

The XJ40, although never produced in massive numbers like mainstream family cars, was made in high numbers for a Jaguar, with over 200,000 built. XJ40s are therefore plentiful and mostly well used – ie probably rough and not worth buying. To avoid wasting time and travel costs you need to ask prepared questions before viewing. Even worn-out examples can still look impressive, so sellers may paint too optimistic a picture unless you focus on specific issues.

View at home or business, not a car park.

Avoid general questions such as asking if the body is 'good.' Ask instead if there is rust on the lower doors, in the sill seams and end caps, or rust around the wheelarches or screen bases etc. In fact feel free to ask where the rust is, rather than if there is any. If the seller says there is no rust, be persistent and explain that it is extremely common if not universal for XJ40s to rust; is the seller really claiming their car has none at all? This may elicit an admission that perhaps there is a little here and there, which opens up the discussion. Fewer sellers will misrepresent a car when questioned directly, since doing so causes trouble if you come to view. The credibility and attitude of the seller will hopefully become apparent during such questioning, which no reasonable person should object to.

Where is the car?
Once you start looking for anything other than a rare model, such as a TWR Jaguar Sport, hopefully you won't need to travel too far to see a selection of cars. If buying from a specialist dealer, even long distance, you should be able to get an excellent picture of the car by telephone and emailed photos. Avoid cars from salted road

or maritime areas unless they have been stored every winter – the XJ40 rusts quickly enough without help from road salt. By the mid 80s, emissions requirements and other regulatory issues were in full force, so usually buying from your own state or country makes most sense to avoid having to alter the car to pass inspection.

Dealer or private sale?

Ask specifically about any damage.

Typically, some of the biggest XJ40 risks concern bodywork and structural rust, as with other older cars. Electrical issues can also be expensive to track down and fix, as can some mechanical problems on V12s. A good dealer should only offer solid cars for resale, although Jaguar club advertisements also contain many good private sales. Not surprisingly, the more you pay the better the car – especially from long-established Jaguar specialists with reputations to protect. The cars are often eligible for some kind of warranty cover that can be worth taking out, which is rarely possible to arrange with a private seller. Dealers usually

Traders normally reject poor cars.

also offer finance, which is another good reason for using them if you want to buy a higher-priced car. However, if you need finance just to buy the car, be sure your budget can stretch to repair, service and fuel costs.

The dealers buy and sell through trade auctions and you can do the same, where usually a 24 hour warranty is supplied (see Chapter 10). For the very cheapest cars, private sales are normally best – especially from long term owners or fellow enthusiasts who have looked after the car with pride. Avoid major work or rebuild projects unless you know what you are doing.

When phoning an advertiser, simply ask about 'the car,' to see if they are selling more than one. This doesn't guarantee they are a trader, but it's a strong indication. Once you have discussed the car, ask how long they have owned it and what papers they have. Good ownership involves significant maintenance, so they should have either receipts for parts if they have done work themselves, or bills from a service shop. Dealers may know less about a car but should have some documentation.

Condition (body/chassis/interior/mechanicals)
Query the car's condition in as specific terms as possible – preferably citing the checklist items described in Chapter 9.

Viewing arrangements
It's always preferable to view at the seller's business or private home, not at the roadside or a car park. A private seller's name and address should be on the car's documents, so beware excuses for why they aren't. Have at least one viewing in daylight and preferably dry weather to check the paint and body properly. If you have to view in wet weather use the opportunity to check for screen leaks or wet boot or interior carpet.

Reason for sale

Genuine sellers will explain why they are selling. XJ40s are all big cars and mostly fairly thirsty, so given today's fuel prices an owner may simply be selling in order to run a cheaper car. Be careful in case they have just put the car in for an inspection and found lots of expensive problems. Thankfully, nowadays many authorities, such as VOSA in the UK, permit on-line viewing of the reasons for failure, as well as the advisory notices issued at the last test, even if the car passed. Almost as bad is the owner who simply wishes to cut their losses and do the minimum to get the car ready for sale to recoup their outlay. Either way, you can inherit the bills they avoided.

LHD/RHD conversions

XJ40 cars are sold widely, so the transatlantic market which exists for E-types and other rare Jaguars has never developed for these cars beyond a few personal imports/exports. Some Australasian trade exists, and a few come to Europe from Japan, but these don't usually involve steering conversions.

Originality

Originality is desirable, not only in terms of value but also for ease of servicing and trouble-shooting. The XJ40 is a complex car and deviations from standard are normally only a source of trouble, rather than improvements. Almost all will have been subject to regular emissions testing and sign-off, which normally requires that original equipment be retained. Check that your authorities will accept slightly reduced safety or emissions standards if considering a modified car.

Very few XJ40s have been 'lumped' with a non-Jaguar engine, such as an American V8. Any which have will appeal to only a tiny market and are, therefore, generally worth far less to the average buyer.

Matching data/legal ownership

The XJ40 has a modern Vehicle Identification Number (VIN) visible through the screen on a tab, and stamped on the front bulkhead seam, so checking that this matches the legal documentation is easy.

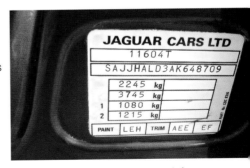

VIN information must match.

Does the vendor own the car outright, is money owed on it, or is it even stolen? Finance checks can often also confirm if the car has ever been a write-off.

In the UK the following organisations supply vehicle data –
HPI – 01722 422 422
AA – 0870 600 0836
DVLA – 0870 240 0010
RAC – 0870 533 3660
Other countries will have similar organisations.

Roadworthiness

Does the car have a roadworthiness or emissions certificate? Test status for UK cars can be checked on 0845 600 5977. Similar checks are available in some other markets. Californian smog-related fittings are generally not required for roadworthiness in other markets. Even many American states will pass a car without the air pump and exhaust gas recirculation equipment or carbon canisters.

Unleaded fuel
All AJ6 and 6.0L V12 engines are designed for unleaded fuel, although depending on local specifications it may be necessary to tune fractionally differently for low-octane fuel. The same applies to 'eco-friendly' fuels with varying proportions of alcohol or hydrocarbon blends which often vary between winter and summer months.

Payment
A cheque will take several days to clear and the seller may prefer to sell to a cash buyer. Cash can also be a valuable bargaining tool but a banker's draft or money order may be acceptable, so ask beforehand.

Buying at auction?
See Chapter 10.

Professional vehicle check
XJ40s are heavy, complicated and usually fast cars, and therefore quicker than most old classics. Consequently, they need to be fully roadworthy for use in modern high-speed traffic. Your local motoring organisation or marque/model specialist will usually conduct a professional examination for a fee. For V12s, try to perform, or pay for, a full compression check. One or two poor cylinders can be missed, even on road test, if you are unfamiliar with V12s.

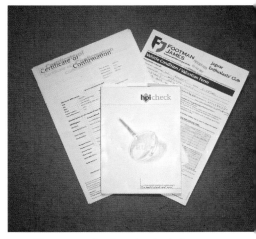

Finance and value checks help.

Other organisations providing car checks in the UK are –
AA – 0800 085 3007 (motoring organisation with vehicle inspectors)
ABS – 0800 358 5855 (specialist vehicle inspectors)
RAC – 0870 533 3660 (motoring organisation with vehicle inspectors)
Other countries will have similar organisations.

6 Inspection equipment
– these items will really help

The most important inspection tool are your eyes, so be sure to bring a good torch and inspect the car at least once in daylight or excellent artificial light. Although the XJ40 does not leak as much as older Jaguars, when checking interiors or the boot/trunk you also need to smell for damp and mould, since damp can arise from blocked air conditioner drains or even leaking brake fluid. The sense of touch also helps when running your fingers over hidden seams or paintwork to detect rust, poorly re-welded flanges and botched filler patches. As for conventional tools, besides the torch you will benefit from taking with you:

This book
A magnet (not too strong) to check for filler
One, or ideally two, trolley jacks to give safe access
Small mirror on a stick for inaccessible areas
Spark tester/inductive timing light and/or spare plug
Probe (a small screwdriver works very well)
Digital camera
A knowledgeable friend

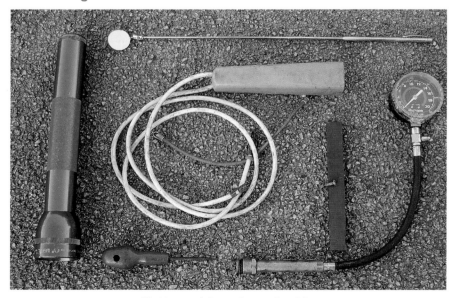

The bare minimum inspection kit.

Useful extras: Compression gauge with long connector (especially for V12s), antifreeze concentration hydrometer, test strips for checking combustion products in coolant (head gasket leak), IR thermometer for checking misfiring cylinders.

There are no fibreglass XJ40 panels so any lack of magnetism will be due to thick filler. A magnet also helps for checking door bottoms, sills, wheelarches and valences. A special tool for checking paint thickness is useful, though not cost-effective for occasional use.

The camera is handy for photographing interiors or external rust areas to get feedback on what is probably needed for repair. Remember that visible corrosion is normally less than hidden rust, although because XJ40s are not the oldest Jaguars, what you see is often closer to what there really is. Nevertheless, apparently mild rust – for example

Jack and stands improve access.

where the sill joins the rear wheelarch – may look minor yet still mean this entire structural area has perhaps rotted from within because of water leaking inside from the rear screen, or through a perforated sill end cap or inner sill to floor seam.

A small screwdriver can be used – with care – as a probe, particularly on the inner and outer sills, chassis sections over the IRS where the mounts attach, and front chassis legs ahead of the subframe (as well as the subframe itself). The sill closing panels inside the wheelarches front and rear should also be solid and can be probed hard since there is no gloss paint involved. The rear lower quarters and both valences are vulnerable and can be probed hard if suspect, since any marks will not be visible. They are not structural, however. A-frame mounts and floors, inner sills, boot floor, and anywhere else that looks rusty should also be probed.

The stick mirror helps check the underside, around the manifolds if the exhaust is blowing, or for seepage from a coolant hose underneath the inlet manifold. A ramp inspection is obviously ideal, but two trolley jacks plus appropriate axle stands can provide viewing room either along one side at a time, or one end at a time.

A dark or shady spot helps visualise any high tension arcing around the distributor, coil or plug wires. To tell if a V12 is running on all cylinders it's good to bring a small in-line or other spark tester or spare plug to use on each plug lead in turn. Not all plugs are equally easy to reach, especially the front two hidden by the air conditioning compressor and the rears behind the throttle pedestal. They need to be checked if there is any doubt, because engines can sometimes run for prolonged periods making seemingly good power with one or more 'dead' cylinders, causing expensive damage. An inductive timing light saves disconnecting any plug wires and can be used to check that the timing is advancing electronically. Read up

A lift inspection is the ideal.

in the handbook how the car's built-in diagnostic computer shows any fault codes present.

If possible, use a test strip to check for the right type and strength of coolant corrosion inhibitors, since neglect in this area – not unusual in frost-free climates – can ruin the internals of the 6-cylinder and especially all-alloy V12 engines. Ideally, you'll also be able to check for signs of combustion gases in the coolant from a faulty head gasket. Both are useful back-up for the usual visual check for bubbling while the engine is running, and smell of exhaust fumes in the coolant. A compression tester is ideal for the most thorough engine check, and accessibility on the sixes couldn't be easier. For the V12 engines it is not a trivial task, so you probably won't be able to do that sort of work until either a final detailed inspection or until you own the car, by which time you are stuck with the results either way. If there is a single test worth paying for in advance, however, it is probably this one.

Show an expert the pictures of any part of the car that concerns you. Ideally, have a friend or knowledgeable enthusiast accompany you: a second opinion is always valuable.

Crooked steering shows up on test.

Road test

More than perhaps most cars, you need to drive a roadworthy XJ40 before buying it. Ask the owner not to start the car beforehand, to check how easily it starts from cold and how well it idles. Listen for engine clatter from the timing chain or top end on start-up. Many fuel-injection problems and fuel or coolant leaks are best checked with a cold engine, before the heat causes liquids to evaporate. The sensor-modulated enrichment or auxiliary air valves can fail. You also need to look for start-up smoke. Check in the mirror if you are driving, or look behind if being driven. A brief puff of blue smoke on the first rev is acceptable, but thereafter the exhaust should be clear or merely clouded with rapidly-clearing water vapour initially. If in the driving seat, press the brake before start-up and check the pedal moves a little further when the engine starts, showing that the servo is working. If the owner insists on driving, ask them to press the brake and watch if it moves.

During an XJ40 road test you will have to try harder to hear noises or sense other problems because the cars are well insulated from road and engine sounds. There should be little or no wind noise up to quite high speeds and, once underway, an XJ40 should ride smoothly without wallowing, clunks or bangs. Sports models on firmer springs/dampers and lower profile tyres ride more firmly though still smoothly. Listen for knocks or whining noises in hubs/suspension and driveline. Anything that feels or sounds like looseness or scraping indicates work is needed – ranging from a slack wheel bearing, worn ball joint or damper bushes to loose differential mounts or damaged universal joint. Elsewhere, catalytic converters or heat shields can rattle, manifolds can crack, and joints come loose due to snapped or missing fasteners.

Any XJ40 should accelerate cleanly and briskly/strongly/very strongly, depending on engine type. There should be no smoke under acceleration once fully warm, or on the overrun, when puffs of blue in the mirror indicate worn guide seals or rings. All engines should be smooth, although the 2.9 and early 3.6 can be coarse. Any car that struggles up hills or overtaking slower vehicles probably needs a tune-up. Full rebuilds are rarely needed.

Check that any cruise control works and ABS and brake pad wear lamps

Drive train noises spell trouble.

don't light during hard braking. Brakes should be powerful and progressive and not pull sideways during this manoeuvre, even with hands-free steering (except for a mild camber effect). If possible, carefully try to brake with one wheel on a loose surface to check the ABS works. Juddering normally indicates warped or corroded discs and/or suspension problems, although it can just be pad deposits on the discs from holding brakes on after a hard stop. The XJ40 has anti-dive geometry but still dips in a firm stop. Bottoming out probably hints at tired springs or shock absorbers, which can be confirmed with a ride height check or 'bounce' test. Make several

Check that the air conditioning works.

low-speed full-lock turns to check for wheel rubbing or power steering noises. V12s or sport models with Powrlok limited slip differentials may creak a little from the rear at full lock. Check the handbrake works and releases fully, especially if it has been little used. It should hold the car on a hill and, although it may need a good pull, should grip well after just a few clicks.

The sixes are smooth and swift in larger sizes, but if you are not used to the power and smoothness of the V12 an apparently well-performing car may actually be misfiring or concealing other substantial faults. The V12 engine is extremely durable and easily covers 200,000 miles with proper oil and coolant changes but must not be allowed to overheat. Try an envelope or loosely folded paper behind the tailpipes during idling to amplify any 'off-beat' rhythm or low-speed misfires, although few engines idle perfectly. Indicated oil pressure and temperature on modern Jaguars should be fairly consistent hot or cold, even on twelves. The manual gearboxes should be silent in all ratios and depressing the clutch should not cause any screeching, though a faint release bearing noise can occur. The auto boxes, especially the post-1990 electronic autos, should change almost imperceptibly.

Check every single minor and electrical control because fixing them can be a nuisance. Some heat and ventilation controls are actuated by vacuum, so you will probably hear a soft movement of air and a faint tap or clonk as the flaps move shortly after the controls are adjusted. Central locking and window switches may have a sluggish or absent movement but often this is through lack of use. Be sceptical of any claim that non-functioning refrigeration merely means the air conditioning needs re-gassing, as the problem is usually more serious.

A tidy engine bay is encouraging.

Checks back at base

If all seems well you're ready delve further. When the engine and transmission are fully warm, move the auto gear selector through all positions 2-3 times, and leave the engine idling while you pull the dipstick and clean/re-insert to check the fluid level is correct for the hot markings. If the fluid is brown instead of red, or smells burnt, this shows lack of maintenance. Look for oil leakage near the distributor, or from the cam cover sides or plug recesses, and listen for a blowing exhaust manifold, grumbling power steering pump, or whining idler pulleys. On V12s, exhaust leaks are problematic due to difficult access.

General condition

XJ40s are not high value cars, so apart from pride of ownership there is little incentive to spend much on them. Keeping what you buy looking good makes more sense than throwing a lot of money at restoring a rough car. Any car that looks immaculate has probably (but not invariably) been also well-treated mechanically.

Body and interior

Is the leather supple and unmarked? Base models have tweed or half-leather upholstery, but apart from curiosity value these will prove hard to sell and should be avoided. Are the electronic instruments and warning lamps all operating correctly? Does the vehicle computer show any codes (read the manual for full operating instructions)? Are the door pulls clean and un-cracked and the veneer unmarked, with the under-dash panels firmly in place?

Are the boot lining and wheel cover present and correctly fitted, and the boot dry with no leaks from the lid or fuel filler? Check for a toolkit, bagged cantilever jack and wheel brace. Is the electric aerial jammed or the body grommet split/missing?

Are panel gaps good with no door drop – especially on the driver's door? Is there rust bubbling around the screens or traces of water damage inside? Headlinings drop less than those on earlier Jaguars, but it still happens. Sunroof operation, rust and leakage should be checked.

Clean, but not everyone's ideal!

XJ40s were built just before rust-proofing became seriously effective so you must inspect the bodywork closely. This is the most expensive, time consuming and skill-dependent aspect of the car to rectify if in poor condition. Even with a V12 it may be better to purchase a car with suspect mechanicals in a confirmed good body, than take on a structurally questionable XJ40 with good running gear.

Does the car sit right, with no corner lower than any other? Under the bonnet, does all look tidy and corrosion free? Does the bonnet hold itself open and look dent free from inside as well as outside, showing no filler has been used?

Try to see as much of the underside as possible – ideally on a lift. The floor and chassis rails should be black or body colour over stonechip, normally with good underseal on top. Check sills for filler – especially in front of and behind the doors, where they meet the bulkheads and along the lower

Top quality tyres suggest care.

inside seam with the floor. The front of the footwells is another weak spot, so lift the carpets to check.

Pull the wheels to and fro hard at the top as a preliminary check for slack bearings or worn suspension/drive universals or output bearings. With the bonnet open, reach in through the driver's window to turn the steering while you view the steering rack body for movement. Look at tyres for unusual wear, indicating suspension or alignment problems. Look for split or crumbling suspension bushes at all pivots or attachment points, especially the A-frame bushes and upper front damper mounts. Check for leaks from the differential input and output seals. Oil mist around the differential breather is normal. Oil leaking from the bell housing can also be gearbox oil but the smell is noticeably different, and in both cases the engine has to come out for a repair. If a check engine light or brake warning light shows, use the Vehicle Condition Monitor controls to the right of the steering wheel to display a code. Codes are listed in the Owner's Manual in some markets, or the Haynes Manual (see Chapter 16) or on www. jag-lovers.org. Pre-90 and post-90 models have different ABS' systems and different warning/test schedules that are beyond the scope of this book. The VCM also highlights which, if any, fuses are blown.

Enthusiast cars are usually good.

Beware 'pimped' custom cars.

8 Key points
– where to look for problems

Key aspects to check on XJ40s are:

Structural bodywork
Instruments and electrics
Transmission, suspension and brakes
Engine condition
Interior trim

Bodywork

The XJ40 cars are all monocoque (frameless) construction so most of the common rust areas affect the integrity of the structure directly or indirectly. Although rust-proofing improved on later cars, even these are by now often

A car for all seasons and journeys.

seriously corroded, so a thorough appraisal is vital.

Because these cars are not very valuable there is no point bothering with a badly rusted car except for emotional reasons, since serious corrosion can cost as much to repair as the car is worth – sometimes more.

If rust has been repaired you need to check the type and extent of corrosion and assume there may still be some hidden rust such as that from condensation in box-sections. The repair is more likely to have been a cheap patch than a full structural cut-back with new press-formed sections inserted. Polyester filler is often used to hide cheap techniques, making it impossible to know how the metal was prepared before being covered with filler and paint.

The XJ40 has bonded screens, although the rubber seals and trim around them can give trouble and allow water to collect and rust around the base. This

Corner damage spoils many cars.

is both unsightly and tricky to repair and is therefore often left too late, with perforation the result. Unfortunately, if water leaks in, it can puddle lower down, from where it can quietly rust the floor pan or under the seats. It can ruin the critical corners where the sills meet the stiffening body sections at the rear wheelarches or the base of the A-posts in front of the doors, and can even spoil electrics under the seats in late cars. Rotting from the inside out means that by the time you see bubbling it is too late for a simple fix. Other common rust traps are the boot lid and bonnet edges, front wing extremities and inner wings.

Electrics

The XJ40 bristled with innovative electronics at launch and even when new some gremlins occurred, especially with the digital dashboard. Twenty years later the problems have become more common, but fortunately they are fairly obvious if you methodically work through all the car's systems and controls. All have fuel injection and electronic ignition, and an on-board computer monitoring system which shows fault codes without a scanner, although the system is not as sophisticated as current on-board diagnostics. Most problems are due to loose connections, dirty switch contacts or broken individual components which

Spoiled varnish, loose trim – ugh!

are normally easy to check by substitution, once you have narrowed down the options and obtained good replacements. Relays are often packaged four to a single module, so one failure means replacing four relays. Check that the full range of controls and gadgets operate correctly, and check the engine harness wiring for brittleness and cracks.

Transmission, suspension and brakes

The transmissions are dependable 4-speed automatics or 5-speed manuals, with electronic control on the post 1990 4-litre models and the 6.0L. Apart from fluid checks when hot it is mostly only possible to check for smooth gear selection and listen for excessive whine or knocks on hard acceleration, harsh shifting, slipping clutches, or to/fro clunking of loose mountings. The post 1990 manuals switched from the separate bell housing 265/262 Getrag to the stronger 290 which continued to the end of the next generation of XJ6 variants in 1997. Most parts for the entire power train are long-lasting and readily available. The strong differential is normally good for further work after new seals, but the rubber Jurid coupling at its nose can break up.

Low fluids = poor maintenance.

The brakes are likewise sturdy and dependable unless neglected or underused, whereupon pins and pistons can become sticky or discs rust. Suspension dampers and rubber components wear eventually, as do the universal joints if not greased routinely. Cars with self-levelling suspension have often been converted to conventional dampers. Apart from track rod ends and front wheel bearings, most suspension repairs need some expertise or special tools to fix. The difficulty of working on them means you probably need to budget for professional refurbishment, although with good tools and care, it is all repairable by the home mechanic.

Engines

All Jaguar engines are inherently durable, but overheating or other neglect can cause problems. For the V12s there is no substitute for a compression test – which is tricky with the crowded location on the 6.0L. A good car from a dealer should be OK but a car with signs of possible neglect requires careful evaluation. The sixes are simpler, very strong and even an engine blow-up is not a total disaster, as a replacement used engine is cheap due to low demand. Mild oil leaks from cam covers etc are common but heavy losses require investigation. There should be no coolant leaks or white powdery deposits from former seepage. Throttle bodies and linkages should be clean with unworn bushes.

Interiors

The interior of an XJ40 is normally a mixture of man-made and natural materials and their survival depends on how they have been treated. They wear well but are expensive to repair, either in material or labour costs, or both, unless you find matching good secondhand parts. The commonest damage is to the driver's seat bolster. Dropped headlining or loose armrests or door cards, loose dash trim, split seat seams, cracked or lifted veneer are all common after 20 years, as are torn or holed carpet and split vinyl. Check for musty smells from water leaks and sickly sweet smells from leaked coolant or hydraulic fluids.

Steve Woodward's 2.9.

9 Serious evaluation

– 60 minutes for years of enjoyment

You need to inspect your lead candidate car(s) thoroughly to decide on purchase and price. Tick the appropriate box for each check and total the points. Be realistic where bodywork is concerned and vigilant for V12 engine faults.

Overall stance

Ex [4] Gd [3] Av [2] Po [1]

If the car has self-levelling suspension, ask that it be left overnight before you arrive, to see if the rear rises slightly on start-up. Once running (or at any time if no SLS is fitted) an XJ40 should sit flat and level front to back and side to side, or very slightly higher at the rear, especially with low fuel load (check the gauge). The heavy V12 can sag at the front also, and thus be level, but low. Note that cars with SportsPack suspension or low-profile tyres on standard wheels will sit lower.

Bryan Neish's perfectly level Sovereign.

On level ground the bottom of the front subframe should be about 160mm above ground with 215 width tyres and 155mm with 205s. An easier but less precise method is to measure from the top of the wheelarch through the centre of the wheel to the ground. Unladen with half a tank of petrol, a normal car will sit around 660-665mm high at this point, and again, level or slightly higher at the rear.

Slightly higher at the rear is OK.

Body panels

Ex [4] Gd [3] Av [2] Po [1]

A good XJ40 should have undistorted panels with even shut lines and the doors following the body contours not sticking out at the base. Look for filler bulges along the bottom of doors or wings and around the headlamps, arches and sills. Feel the wheelarch returns for rough metal or double thickness or seams from repairs, especially at the lower front area of the rear sills. Loose or missing mud shields in the front wheelarch can hide rot, so clean and inspect by torchlight. The area around the filler flap can suffer badly and the radiator support crossmember is an inspection fail if unsound, but may not be visible with the undertray in place.

Hans Goerlitzer's perfect panel gaps.

Underside and sills

The front footwell corners around the jacking points rust easily, where stone chips allow water behind the underseal. Check from inside and outside the car and try to lift the car on the jack to check for creaking/buckling if possible. Beware of thick underseal, over poor welding or bad steel. The inner sill floor seam rusts in a neat line, compromising shell strength significantly. A-frame attachment points are normally not too bad but the rear lower quarters can be, although they are not structural. Check for rust in the chassis

Check sills for rot under seals.

rails within about a foot any front or rear suspension mount and if the front or rear screen bases are perforated then walk away, as the water will have rotted inside the lower chassis angles too. The front upper section of the sills is hidden behind the wings but water and mud can collect here behind the splash panel and rot down from above.

Bonnet, inner wings and boot

The front edge of the bonnet rots from the inside out and even light bubbling means rust within. Headlight areas do not rust as badly as earlier Jaguars but make sure each lamp is solid

to the push. Look for evidence of accident repairs, rippling on the main chassis rails or patching on the inner wings, especially around the damper mount or holes used to secure wheelarch liners. The upper rear corners where the inner wing meets the scuttle can soak in wet debris, trapping water and perforating and the heater intake plenum can let water into the cabin. Top shock absorber mounts can be checked, as can the battery tray area on pre-'93 cars.

The bootlid rusts from inside at the rear top and lower edges and under the tactile panel. The boot itself rusts if a seal is bad or water enters through a cracked aerial grommet. Major electrical components in the boot can suffer from damp too.

Perfect underfloor.

Typical sill and jacking point rust.

Wings and sills rot together.

Bad wheelarch repair.

Floors

The carpets and underlay must be lifted back to check the inner sill seams, seat belt

Daylight visible through the floor!

attachments and on late cars the state of the under-seat electrics, which suffer badly from any water under the carpets. The fuse boxes at the base of the A pillars also suffer if kicked or wetted. There should be various plugs in place and no through holes.

Doors

Ex	Gd	Av	Po
4	3	2	1

Check the door gaps and feel along the corners and bottom edges. Door handles, especially in the rear, are notorious for breaking so check each lock works inside and out, as well as the electrical central locking and windows. Probe door apertures for rust at the base of the A, B and C pillars. Door drop normally only affects the driver's door, so lift it to check for slack, and look for heavy strike marks on the latch components, as well as a loose/damaged door card or armrest. Doors should fit flush and close

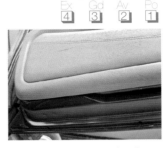

Check for rust under the doors.

with a thud not a clang. Perimeter seals should be intact and can be checked by closing the door onto a sheet of paper at the top and front of the window frame.

Petrol tanks and pipework

Ex	Gd	Av	Po
4	3	2	1

The petrol tank is generally trouble free inside the dry boot, unlike earlier XJ series, but check for fuel smells in the boot and a filler recess drain blocked with leaf debris or split from age. Look for signs the boot trim has been disturbed during remedial work of some sort. It is often replaced shoddily and in the wrong order, with unsightly seams or oily fingerprints left behind. Front boot trim panel removal suggests fuel tank repairs (or pump trouble on later cars). Right trim damage suggests ECU or electric aerial problems and left cover damage suggests fuel filler solenoid issues or leakage problems. For 93/94 battery-in-boot models, lift the cover to check a full size battery is fitted. The trim fasteners are, more often than not missing. Examine the spare tyre for heavy or uneven wear, suggesting possibly recent suspension bush or alignment issues.

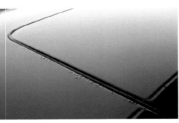

Check sunroof for closure and rust.

Sunroof

Ex	Gd	Av	Po
4	3	2	1

Check for rust around the sunroof opening and examine for movement, greased channels and intact lifting mechanism. Headliner stains suggest blocked drains or a poor seal around the hatch.

Paint

Ex	Gd	Av	Po
4	3	2	1

Various types of paint were used, each with good and bad points. Thermoplastic paints were troublesome in some hot climates and, due to low value, an XJ40 is less likely to receive top class paint repairs than a more expensive Jaguar. Many are, therefore, patched and blown over, or given a poor full spray. This can be forgiven since good paint can cost more than the car and is one reason to shop for the best you can afford. Check for overspray inside

Worn/bleached paint is bad news.

wheelarches or on rubber aperture seals and cable sheaths into doors. Look for poor finish inside the fuel filler recesses, along the tops of the inner wings where the outer panels bolt on, and under the front and rear bumpers. See also Chapter 14.

Lights & body trim

Ex	Gd	Av	Po
4	3	2	1

The large rectangular lamps and quad lamps are both controlled by electronic modules, so check all beams function as intended. Beware cracked glass or rusted reflectors which result from stone chip holes, as the large lamps are expensive to replace. Rear lamp lenses can fade or crack from bumps, and the long bright trims on each bumper are easy to bend with parking contact. Even if the 3-piece chrome trims are intact (many rust from underneath) the beams underneath can bend and

Rear lenses crack and fade.

look unsightly as the rubber facings sit crooked. Headlamp washer covers often fall off.

Some cars will have chrome door trim or extra boot trim which looks nice to some but is often the first to deteriorate. At least most door impact trims should be stick-on, not riveted. Stainless window trims usually survive well but many boot badges do not and make the car look shabby if corroded.

Expensive lights should be unbroken.

Rear bumper fog lights are vulnerable to parking damage and the fronts, if fitted, to stone chip cracking.

Body seals

Ex	Gd	Av	Po
4	3	2	1

The XJ40 was a quiet car, due to good sealing around doors and windows. Furflex door aperture trim is largely decorative, but, if falling off the cant rail area or vertical sections, can let in noise and looks unsightly. The top of the engine compartment has a transverse seal that often harbours rust on the front scuttle seam just ahead of the wipers. Screen seals are critical, even though the glass itself is bonded, and many cars will show signs of water entry, perishing or rust, and this needs to be factored into refurbishment plans. It can easily rule a poor car out, as repairs are not trivial.

Door seals should be intact.

Rust is common under the scuttle seal.

Wheels and tyres

Ex	Gd	Av	Po
4	3	2	1

Most XJ40s were supplied with 15in wheels, steel on base models (where sold). The V12 and some Sports models used 16in rims and lower profile tyres to match, and could be specified by the customer as an extra on other cars too. Steel

Special correct 'J-suffix' Pirellis.

wheels used full-coverage silver plastic trims, which are more expensive to buy new than a used set of alloys, so many cars have been upgraded. Wheels from a later 1994-2003 X300 car can make an XJ40 look younger. Original high-profile 65-section 225 section tyres give the best ride and speedometer accuracy and must be the correct rating and condition for such a heavy and fast car. Later 60 or 55 section tyres on 16in rims give better steering but a less plush ride. Discount heavily for metric wheels unless tyres are new, since tyres are expensive and hard to find.

Worn down to steel from excess toe-out.

Ex	Gd	Av	Po
4	3	2	1

Exhaust

All XJ40 cars used twin exhausts with characteristic rolled-edge trims. The system is large and expensive, with catalysts on all North American cars and eventually all others too. Middle silencer substitute pipes are a cost-effective alternative to expensive OEM parts, but at the price of slightly worse noise and refinement. Check that the rear silencers do not knock the bodywork at the sides of the recess or where the tailpipes emerge under the rear valance. The over-axle

Beware metric wheels.

pipes get neglected because of access difficulties, so ensure these are good. The thin cast-iron manifolds can crack and give a characteristic blowing sound, and manifold to down pipe joints can work loose, but since they mostly use large metal olives it is often enough merely to tighten any loose nuts to regain a seal. There should be no hissing or blowing noises, which would indicate a failed gasket or stripped studs etc, especially on V12s.

Even factory stainless rots eventually.

Ex	Gd	Av	Po
4	3	2	1

Glass and wipers

Screens give little trouble, although the heated front screens often fail on one or both sides due to switch, wire or relay problems. The rear heated screen is robust unless heavy objects are carried on the parcel shelf and damage it.

The single wiper system ensures little lift at speed, but the increased wiper speed over the glass causes faint scratching due to grit under the arc of the wiper blade. At each service the dealer was supposed to polish the screen with a special glass paste and fit a new wiper blade, but on older cars this is usually not done and the faint dull scratching

One side failed on heated screen.

can be a nuisance at night. Switch gear is robust but check that the intermittent wipe and washers both work.

Rear suspension & brakes

Ex 4 Gd 3 Av 2 Po 1

No rust, but is any oil left inside?

The XJ40 featured a new independent rear suspension designed to give better location for the differential and allowing

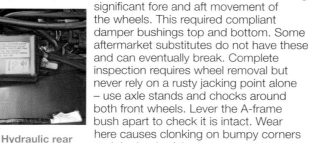

Hydraulic rear suspension can break.

significant fore and aft movement of the wheels. This required compliant damper bushings top and bottom. Some aftermarket substitutes do not have these and can eventually break. Complete inspection requires wheel removal but never rely on a rusty jacking point alone – use axle stands and chocks around both front wheels. Lever the A-frame bush apart to check it is intact. Wear here causes clonking on bumpy corners and the back of the car moves about. Sometimes a small stone can get lodged

Check universal joints for play.

Parts removed to fit normal dampers.

between the A-frame and the floor and give a mysterious rattle or tapping noise but normally it is the shock absorber bushes or valving that have failed. Check the wheel bearings for play or grinding, or play in the universal joints, which act as both driveshaft and suspension links. Slight diff output shaft end float is acceptable, but anything over 1mm is not, especially if the seals are leaking. V12s had a limited slip differential as standard and strange creaking from the rear on tight slow turns normally means the

limited slip oil additive is missing.

The handbrake cable should not bind and be lubricated and unfrayed. Handbrake shoes cannot be inspected without rear disc removal, which themselves should be largely corrosion free and without ridges.

It is difficult to check for play at the various inner rubber pivots and outer roller bearings, but a tyre lever and some judicious prying will reveal serious play. Good signs are fresh grease on all nipples. Check the fuel filter in front of the left rear wheel to see if the pipes look rusty or the filter has been changed recently.

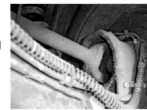

Check rear hub carriers and bearings.

Front suspension, brakes & steering

Ex 4 Gd 3 Av 2 Po 1

XJ40 cars had a separate front subframe with rubber chassis vee mounts. This subframe can rust badly because many are filled with foam (for refinement/noise damping reasons) which acted like a sponge. Powder coating also meant that

Front spring pans can rust through.

Weeping power steering.

apparently intact areas of paint were actually loose sheets of plastic and water was creeping underneath by capillary action and causing invisible rust. Prod very hard all over it, as the scratches will not be seen and this is an important safety area, with replacement the only remedy. The long plush springs may hide a broken coil. Wishbone bushings can be visually inspected for perishing or swelling and play is easiest to check if the car is lowered onto spring pan supports so the suspension is in its normal orientation at mid-laden position. Dampers can be visually inspected for top or bottom mount break-up or fluid leakage. Bounce each corner to check for damper condition.

Oil-rotted anti-roll bar and wishbone pivots.

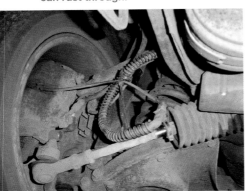

Bodged lines and wires.

Check all ball joints for split gaiters and slack, and the anti-roll bar rubbers and drop links. Have someone turn the steering wheel while you feel for play at the track rod ends and look for rack movement in the bushings. This is serious because the rack bushes cannot be replaced alone and a complete refurbished rack is required. Look for oil leaks from the power steering gear, although a wet rack is often caused by engine oil rather than steering leaks. There are heat shields which need to be present on V12s to prevent exhaust heat from damaging the rack.

Whilst under the car, inspect the large bottom radiator hose and the radiator core and support bushings. Check the vented front discs for scoring and adequate pad thickness and wired caliper bolts on pre-1990 cars. Check for signs of cracked flex hoses or rusted brake pipes. The brake reservoir should have clean fluid without sediment. There are simple checks for the two different types of ABS system which are beyond the scope of this book. See www.jag-lovers.org and search the XJ40 forum.

Good damper bushes. Many crumble.

Ex	Gd	Av	Po
4	3	2	1

Cabin trim

Even base model XJ40s have fully trimmed cabins and a poor interior is a reason for walking away unless you happen to have access to good secondhand parts

Pristine Daimler Insignia trim.

Mild driver's seat damage.

and the time to switch everything. Musty smells mean water leaks from somewhere. Console tops are vinyl on base models and can

Badly refitted trim. Electrical problems?

split or wear through. Consoles today often have holes or cuts where mobile phones were fitted. All cars used veneered dashboards which are harder wearing than older Jaguars and should be in good condition. Headliners by now can be sagging and are awkward to replace, although sometimes problems can be fixed by dropping only the front or rear and working behind the board to reattach it. Unless you have a special reason, do not buy a car with anything other than leather seats, as this is what people expect in a Jaguar. All this style of seat facing was leather although apart from Daimler/VDP models, much of the less obvious trim such as side seat panels and door handles etc was Ambla – Jaguar's very convincing leather substitute. Check any picnic trays work smoothly.

Carpets

The carpets lie above moulded foam underlays. Sound-deadening anti-drum material is used extensively and can trap liquids. Check for brake fluid leakage around the pedals, water from blocked AC drains in the centre or from screen leaks at the sides. New carpets can hide terrible floors so lift to check. High-wear areas are vinyl faced but look for a car that has been used with floor mats so that the carpet is still good.

Ex Gd Av Po
[4] [3] [2] [1]

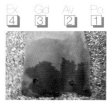

Soaked front foam underlay.

Instruments and electrics

Ex Gd Av Po
[4] [3] [2] [1]

Early XJ40s came with a futuristic electronic dashboard with a mini TV-type display. Later versions reverted to conventional instruments for reliability but kept an on-board diagnostic and fault alert facility, operated together with a trip computer

Check every single control.

Test all seat motors.

from the right finger board beside the steering wheel. Look for any missing or broken warning lamp bulbs when you first turn the key before actually starting the car. Dead bulbs can hide a warning. When the engine is running all warnings should extinguish.

Depending on model there is a huge range of switches/sensors/relays, etc, and the only way to check is to operate every electrical function listed in the handbook. If fuse covers look recently disturbed, or there is insulating tape or a blown fuse in the ashtray be suspicious of electrical hassles. Most relays are in four-pack boxes and one failed component for a rarely-used function can necessitate replacing all associated relays in the same box. The later the car, the better the electrics. Familiarize yourself with the location of all relays and fuses. Examine the general condition of any visible wiring. Check the blowers work correctly each side as water can ruin them and they are hard to repair.

All XJ40 cars use a negative earth alternator system with battery gauge (actually a voltmeter) to monitor charging and battery condition. The basic charging system is reliable. Many problems are due to corroded fuses and fuse-holders, poor earths, damaged wiring and malfunctioning switches, most of which can be remedied easily with patience, a good wiring diagram, and some small tools and contact cleaner. Other systems, such as the main ECU, are very reliable, but in case of trouble you either need a competent auto-electrician or the ability to try substituting known good parts on a trial basis, until the fault is eliminated.

Torn seals and connectors are common.

Cooling system

The XJ40 cooling system is modern and more reliable than older Jaguars, so overheating is uncommon. Nevertheless, it still relies on proper servicing and maintenance, and, if neglected, it can cause poor running or even serious engine damage. The plastic header tank serves an easily accessible water pump that can be grasped to feel for spindle wear. Look for fresh gaskets or hose clamps indicating

Ex 4 Gd 3 Av 2 Po 1

Collapsed radiator bushes.

recent replacement. The hose under the inlet manifold is a particularly tricky one to work on but is very important and can destroy the engine if it blows at high speed. Hoses should be sound, with no corrosion around the alloy spigots. The top hose carries the hottest water and suffers first but if replaced alone others may then fail from age. A V12 has very many hoses and replacing them is a major task that should appear in the service record – otherwise assume most if not all need renewing.

Check for fan cracks and pump leaks.

On 2.9, 3.6 and V12 engines check the base of the engine-driven fan blades for cracks. A cold fan clutch should stop spinning after about half a turn if flicked round. Additional electric fans are fitted to some cars, including most with air conditioning, or the 3.2 and 4.0 cars which use electric fans exclusively. Let the engine idle and check the fans cycle on and off correctly. Some people wire the fans to be on permanently but this should not be needed. Look at the long bolts in the thermostat housing on sixes and see if there is heavy corrosion, as they have a habit of seizing or snapping when you need to change a thermostat. Excessive use of leak sealants can build up and block radiator passages, as do rust and scale when the wrong coolant has been used. Is the coolant clean and fresh-looking?

Fuel system

Ex	Gd	Av	Po
4	3	2	1

Fuel leaks show up best on cold starts.

All models use fuel injection and a complete fuel injection system check needs special equipment, but you can look for hardened rubber fuel hoses or signs of fuel weeping, which is normally most obvious on a cold engine when cranking, before warm metal causes the fuel to evaporate and appear dry. Injector connectors should be unbroken and firmly held by spring clips, with the wires not split or cracked where they emerge, or indeed anywhere else in the engine harness, which becomes brittle with age, especially on the V12 cars. The main fuel filter is out of sight down by the back wheel but some add an extra filter in the engine compartment.

Engine

Ex	Gd	Av	Po
4	3	2	1

The AJ6 is an immensely strong engine and rarely breaks. It was the world's first all-alloy, mass-produced, in-line, 24V six cylinder car engine. Brief rattling on start up from cold is acceptable but correctly adjusted Jaguar engines should run with just a light rustle from the valve gear, once warm. Loud tapping is potentially a fiddly valve adjustment or a broken chain guide or worse. Look inside the oil filler cap to see if there is creamy 'mayonnaise' – a sure sign of frequent cold running or a coolant leak.

The mighty 6.0L is reliable.

Some whirring from the timing chains is permissible but metallic clatter is not. Screeching noises can be a loose belt or worn pulley bearing, but need to be confirmed. The exhaust note should be regular and even at idle, although some hunting is common. With clean oil and coolant – easily checked – any XJ40 engine should last many years. The 2.9 engines share the same bottom end as the 3.6 and were made for tax reasons in some large European markets. Even at the factory the engine was not liked and always struggled to propel the heavy car. A 2.9 should not be high on your list except for curiosity reasons, as better options are easily available. Obvious fuel smell on the dipstick or exhaust smell in the header tank is a bad sign. There is no substitute for a full compression check if there is any question about an engine's health. Having said that, if it sounds right, looks right and goes right, it probably *is* right.

Transmission

Ex	Gd	Av	Po
4	3	2	1

Most XJ40s were ZF 4-speed automatics, with a Getrag 5-speed available outside North America and the V12 using a GM truck gearbox for durability. All transmissions are generally reliable but not everlasting. It is therefore wise to keep money in reserve if buying a particularly high mileage example or one with a tow bar. Provided fluid is kept clean and topped up (check for brown discolouration and burnt smell) they can go for 100,000 plus miles but will eventually require some attention. Fluid level should only be checked when fully warmed up after a good run, and after moving through all the gear selector positions twice, to fill the valve block passages and avoid a falsely

Good transmission, soggy mount.

high reading. The first to second change is imperceptible on a good automatic and happens at slow speeds normally, with the second to third change happening soon afterwards on light throttle, but available on kickdown. Check that the torque converter lock-up operates at around 50-52mph as it should, and can be noticed by a slight drop in revs at that point on a light throttle. Dismiss any car with obvious drive problems such as noises or failure to move off immediately, especially if there is plenty of fluid.

Manual gearboxes are not the slickest but not bad. Sometimes a shrieking noise accompanies clutch disengagement, due to a worn or dry pilot bearing in the flywheel, which supports the nose of the input shaft. Ditto a dry release bearing. The sound disappears when the clutch is released but eventually gets worse and is a big job to repair. The clutch on manual cars is moderately heavy and long but should engage and disengage quickly and smoothly. The small reservoir above the pedal box often has a snapped top due to ham-fisted over-tightening. Ugly dark fluid or weeping pipework are sure signs of neglect. Clutch master cylinder rebuild kits are no longer available from Jaguar – only the complete cylinder and reservoir assembly. Slave cylinder kits do exist, so a weep underneath is not the end of the world. Fluid on the carpet or along the lines and besides the bell housing suggest present or past leaks. The clutch and brake and throttle pedals each have return springs but these are often broken so check for lazy or sloppy action.

Oil leaks and pressure

Ex 4 Gd 3 Av 2 Po 1

All XJ40 engines use proper garter-type seals at the back of the crankshaft, so leakage from the bell housing is less common than previously. Other leaks are easily fixable, which means a very oily car has been neglected. The cam cover breather can clog and the throttle body may drip if it has not been cleaned in years. One common oil leak on the AJ6 engine is from a gallery in the head joint near the distributor. This can leak badly, requiring head removal to fix. V12s have a common leak from the timing cover inspection plug but should have no leaks from either crank seal or timing chest or breather housing, though oil mist is normal. The 6.0L was the only V12 to use a modern lip seal at the back of the crank. A cracked sump or stripped drain plug on any engine (all too common) will require effort to repair, although drips may just be from a hardened or missing copper washer.

Indicated oil pressure as shown on the damped gauge should settle to mid scale when warm and hardly move thereafter. V12 engines are known for low idle oil pressure – sometimes below 10 psi – but this shows up less on the 6.0L, and in any case is OK provided it climbs immediately when revved.

The power steering reservoir is small and can be read hot or cold on opposite sides of the dipstick, so is easy to check except where accessibility is tricky on V12s. There should be no significant weeping anywhere in the steering system either from the pipework, pump or bellows on the rack, where rack seals wear out. Sometimes steering can very occasionally be alarmingly loose when cold for the first few miles – feeling as if the wheels are disconnected. Walk away from any such car, even if it returns to normal quickly – heavy tyre wear can be a clue that there is serious play somewhere in the rack. Gearbox and differential will last a long time with oil drips, provided the levels are kept topped up.

Distributor and ignition

Ex 4 Gd 3 Av 2 Po 1

The AJ6 distributor serves merely to send the spark to the appropriate plug.

Advance retard and timing are taken care of by the ignition ECU. The Marelli system in the 6.0L is also much more than merely a trigger system, although because of the unusual twin-track rotor and cap design, you should always use original Marelli components to avoid the very rare chance of one bank cutting out and starting a catalyst fire. Note that some engine diagnostics and other electrical issues such as blown fuses can be checked using the Vehicle Condition Monitor (VCM) console on the right of the steering wheel. Full instructions and code meanings are beyond the scope of this book but can be found on www.jag-lovers.org and in the Jaguar manuals.

Check for genuine Marelli parts on V12s.

Evaluation procedure

Add up the total points. Score: **100 = perfect; 75 = good; 50 = average; 25 = buyer beware!** Cars scoring over 70 should be completely useable and require the minimum of repair, although continued maintenance and care will be required to keep them in condition. Cars scoring between 25-51 will require serious restoration (at much the same cost regardless of score). Cars scoring between 52-69 will require very carefull assessment of necessary repair/restoration costs in order to reach a realistic value.

10 Auctions
– sold! Another way to buy your dream

Apart from the JaguarSport models or special editions such as the Majestic or Insignia, XJ40s are only rare if you are looking for a special trim and body colour combination, or a manual. For the cheapest deals, or if searching for a specific model, you may wish to buy at auction.

Auction pros & cons

Pros: Auctions are wholesale/trade markets and priced accordingly. Auctions usually offer certified ownership, freedom from outstanding finance and a chance to check all paperwork and obtain 24hrs warranty.

Cons: You may need to drive far yet lose the bidding. You may only get limited information beforehand and some of that may be open to question. You will probably not be able to test drive the car or even start it up, although by arriving early on preview day you may be able to see the car off-loaded and witness what lengths the seller has to go to in order to coax it to life. The cars are often less

Study auction cars beforehand.

than showroom clean and since XJ40s have not yet reached full 'classic' status the auction is likely to be a general trade affair rather than a high-end classic event with top class cars.

Admission is normally by catalogue for two people, so take a friend. Even if you've tracked down your dream model you need to decide your personal price limit and stop bidding once it goes over, with your friend reminding you to stop, if necessary! Failiure to do so can mean paying far over the odds, and since the buyer's premium increases pro-rata, any problems with the car will seem all the more annoying.

Catalogue prices and payment details

Each auction house publishes terms and conditions and spells out charges and acceptable payment methods in its catalogue. These normally give price estimates for most lots and full or immediate part-payment or a deposit are usually requested, with the balance payable within 24 hours. Look at the small print for cash and credit card limits and options such as personal cheques or debit cards or bank drafts. The car won't be released until paid for, with storage at your cost until completion.

Preview day

Many specialist auctions hold preview days where you can examine the cars away from the feverish auction atmosphere. Auction staff or sellers may start the cars or show you around and you are permitted to look underneath but not jack the car up yourself. So take a torch and possibly a mirror on a stick for a better view.

Auction day
Cars are sold in order of lot number so get there earlier for low number lots. Phrases such as 'It's with me at …' mean the car hasn't yet reached reserve. 'It's for sale at …' means the car has reached reserve and will now sell to the highest bidder. Cars still unsold when the hammer drops may be open to offers via the auctioneer.

eBay & the internet
eBay & other online auctions cover the best and the worst of the auction spectrum. It may be possible to bid across continents yet have a trusted person inspect the car in person and report back to you. Owners clubs and groups such as www.jag-lovers. org are ideal for this, although you should offer payment for their time or expenses and decide that you will trust their advice.

If you are bidding very low and do not mind the resultant car being poor because you have risked so little, then you are on safer ground. The author himself has bought several cheap Jaguars sight unseen and not been disappointed. Tread warily, however! There are far more poor XJ40s being auctioned than there are excellent cars.

Avoid 'flat battery' non-runners.

Most on-line sources show the seller's location, and may even allow you to search by distance from home, which can be useful. Always check, however, that the car is actually at the sellers location. Opinion is divided on whether it is better to choose your upper limit and bid that at the outset, or let yourself be possibly carried away by auction fever, bidding and re-bidding in the dying moments.

Remember, too, that it will be very difficult to obtain satisfaction if a dishonest seller disappears with your money, or a car never arrives because it never existed. On-line payment schemes provide some protection, as does use of a credit card, but the onus will still be on you to do all the running and work hard to recover any losses.

Auctioneers
Barrett-Jackson www.barrett-jackson.com; Bonhams www.bonhams.com; British Car Auctions BCA) www.bca-europe.com or www.british-car-auctions.co.uk; Cheffins www.cheffins.co.uk; Christies www.christies.com; Coys www.coys.co.uk; eBay www.ebay.com; H&H www.classic-auctions.co.uk; RM www.rmauctions. com; Shannons www.shannons.com.au; Silver www.silverauctions.com.

11 Paperwork
– correct documentation is essential!

The right stuff for the right car

Paperwork may be boring, but when buying and selling cars, incorrect or incomplete paperwork can break a deal. The XJ40 is not truly an old car, and even early ones should still have factory handbooks or service paperwork. History files are unlikely to be especially interesting on youngish cars but do make a car more saleable, even if they may not enhance value by very much. Cheap cars with no service history or other paperwork are doubtful prospects, unless you judge their condition or value to be excellent using this book. The seller may convince you they have mislaid

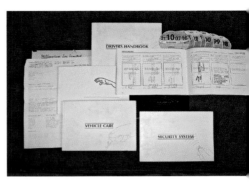

The more history the better.

some documents, but will *you* sound equally convincing later, if you ever sell the car? Unlikely. These cars were mostly originally bought by companies or wealthy individuals and were properly serviced, so 15 years later there should still be some trace of this and a supplying dealer may still be able to provide some background from service records, although data protection legislation can inhibit its release. For the V12s especially, good documentation is almost essential.

Registration documents

Beware a private seller who has only just acquired the car they are selling. Why are they selling on so quickly? Lack of ownership certification normally means extra care is needed with the seller. Where documents do exist, check that serial numbers actually match the car. The XJ40 has a VIN tag visible through the windscreen so checking this is clean and easy. Sellers should issue a signed dated and addressed receipt.

Roadworthiness certificate

Most administrations require that vehicles are regularly tested to prove that they are safe to use. Tests are usually carried out at approved locations and old certificates can confirm the car's history – especially mileage – since dashboards can be changed because of faults, thus altering mileage. Good cars are roadworthy with full paperwork and able to be test driven. Anything less is worth very little.

Road licence

Many countries have an age-related exemption or reduction in taxes but XJ40s are normally too young to qualify for most systems of reduced taxation.

Certificates of authenticity

The Jaguar Daimler Heritage Trust (www.jdht.com) provides Production Record

Trace Certificates (often referred to as 'Heritage Certificates') for a small fee to those who can prove ownership and supply copies of the car VIN and title document. The certificate confirms build and dispatch dates, specification and trim codes, model type, original colours, original selling distributor and sometimes the first owner and registration number.

Valuation certificate

Valuation certificates are rare for such cheap and modern cars, which are usually valued by trade tables like any other. There are lots of examples and even good cars are not that expensive. Such documents may be needed for 'agreed value' insurance but should act only as confirmation of your own assessment, rather than a guarantee of value, because the expert has probably not even seen the car. See Chapter 16 for organisations providing valuations.

Service & restoration history

Few XJ40s will have been fully restored so few will have an extensive history file of work done, although there should be receipts and preferably photographs of major work, and of course servicing.

Items like the original bill of sale, handbook, parts invoices and repair or parts bills all add to the story of the car. Even a correct brochure for the car's model year, or original contemporary road tests, are useful documents.

Paperwork must match the car data plate.

Condition

If the car is suitable you should offer a figure based on the asking price, adjusted by your findings (Chapter 9). Allow for repairing any faults and use price guides in the classic car press to support your offer, based on whatever condition the particular example is in.

Give your offer credibility by providing auction values reported in the press, or eBay prices (which are often helpfully low). Few XJ40 owners think they are sitting on a gold mine but some do have unrealistically high expectations of value, particularly if they bought a few years ago before the model went into price free-fall when even the later and mostly better X300 models became very cheap and plentiful on the used car market. For a non-standard car you'll need to decide which deviations from standard enhance the value and which detract from it.

Desirable options/extras

These are not rare cars, so there is little need to keep them all perfectly original and good prices may be asked for cars that differ considerably from catalogue specification. On the other hand, they have never been cars that begged to be customized so most are still original. There is a market for cars that are totally standard, but many buyers are happy to see changes such as an interior adapted from a more upmarket model like a Daimler or Vanden Plas, a sporting body kit or in-car entertainment upgrades, or special paint and wheels. For some, anything non-standard or missing reduces the value. Others who like to use their cars may prefer sensible enhancements such as a later AJ16 engine – particularly a supercharged version – under the bonnet.

Two very common and useful upgrades are ditching the metric wheels fitted during the eighties and converting any self-levelling suspension cars to standard

Manuals are rare and desirable to some.

damper operation. Sometimes wheels from X300 are fitted, although several 16in wheel designs from the last XJ40s (such as the Kiwi and 20-spoke) carried over to the next series, anyway. A clear upgrade is to fit any Jaguar production alloy wheel to a base model originally sold with steel wheels, as some were in Europe. Likewise, substituting full leather seating for tweed or part-leather, or retro-fitting extras such as cruise control or air conditioning from a higher

Badly-mounted leapers detract.

spec model to an entry-level car, helps value. However, it is generally best to ignore base-level models anyway, since they offer only basic equipment and are harder to resell. You should concentrate on fully specified cars unless you have a very specific reason to do otherwise, such as searching out a manual car (which were often entry-level models).

Standard exhausts were mostly low-grade stainless but need replacing after about ten years, when better 304 grade quality stainless can be fitted. Catalyst substitute pipes are a moot point because although they help fuel mileage slightly, they may make the car technically illegal. In some jurisdictions, so long as the car passes emissions tests there is no problem, and a good car should pass inspection with good lambda feedback operation and minimal catalyst assistance. AJ6 Engineering provides dyno-proven extractor systems for 6s and V12s.

Customisation noise can hurt sales appeal.

All XJ40s have electronic ignition with distributors containing no advance retard mechanism (which is done electronically). A few have custom distributorless ignition systems or combined ignition/injection programmable engine management systems, but unless they have full documentation they can reduce value for subsequent owners. There are handling upgrades available from specialists, such as Harvey Bailey in the UK, or various American outlets, but apart from fitting Jaguar Sport Pack trim or running gear from a sports model, there are limited off-the-shelf tuning or customisation options.

A manual transmission conversion is not everyone's choice for a luxury car but generally is worth having if fuel economy and performance are higher on your list than convenience or purchase price.

Late wheels freshen a car.

Halogen lights are standard, and both 4-lamp and twin rectangular lamp designs were offered. There was a supplier of kits to convert XJ40 body panels as well as lights to the later curvy X300 appearance, but this was a limited business, since the real thing soon became highly affordable secondhand and was a much better car technically as well as visually. Twin lamps can be swapped for quad lamps and vice versa, but it is not a trivial operation. Liquefied gas fuelling conversions (provided a petrol system is left in place) can dramatically reduce running costs and are reasonably common in UK and European XJ40s. You can buy either a complete converted car or convert one with equipment taken from a scrapped XJ40. In the latter case an expert fitting service will be needed unless you know all about LPG. Fitting LPG equipment yourself is unlikely to be cost-effective unless you do over 10-15,000 miles per year.

Undesirable features

Converted former automatics can sometimes take longer to sell because more people expect a Jaguar to be automatic, but the increased economy offered by a carefully-driven manual may gradually change that view as fuel prices move relentlessly upward. Cloth interiors do not sell as well as leather although some do prefer the increased comfort in extremes of heat or cold. Screen leaks and dropped headlinings can make a car almost unsaleable if better examples are available locally. Dull or non-metallic colours generally sell slower than solid colours. A tow bar can spell a hard-worked transmission and often puts off buyers, as can poorly-fitted or non-Jaguar body kits, or excessively large or showy wheels and exhausts.

Cruise and upgrades add value.

XJ40 cars are sufficiently modern that it is probably easier, cheaper and quicker to search out a good example than try to rectify significant faults on a poor car. There will be plenty to keep you occupied even on a good car, but setting out to repair a car that is already in need of major work is certainly not cost-effective and unlikely to be

It is best to buy a good car initially.

especially satisfying either, unless you obtain the car for very little, or you want to learn your way around Jaguars.

Restoring an XJ40 is nothing like repairing a simple older car, as there are lots of electronic component and circuit faults which can't be diagnosed, much less repaired, without specialist knowledge and some equipment. This puts them in a different class to simpler cars from an earlier era which are never likely to disappoint an owner due to spiralling costs or complexity of repair. If you have never restored a car before, you would be well-advised to learn the necessary skills on something simpler and cheaper and of lower performance potential.

Because XJ40s are 'aspirational' purchases for some, a lot of cars are bought on emotion, which have an apparently clean exterior that hides a rotten body smartened up to sell. If you already have such a car, or have decided to buy one in

Can you handle a sea of warning lights?

need of work, or even know where you can obtain one for free, ask yourself whether it makes sense. The cars are rarely, if ever, worth what they cost to restore so it normally makes far more sense to buy one in decent condition and avoid major work. By the same token, you should think twice before taking on a car with, for example, a great and inviting interior or engine but terminal rot below the waistline. One look into the leather and wood interior of a clean car can cause buyers to be over-optimistic about the scope and difficulty of the metalwork repairs which may lie hidden under apparently superficial rust.

Whilst the 6-cylinder engines are not too hard to work on, the big V12 is bulky and complex and can swallow a lot of specialist hours to refurbish properly. Thankfully, most are still in good condition, but this is by no means assured after 14-15 years of possibly variable maintenance.

Think about the type of work you are realistically capable of, then calculate the likely budget for a professional doing the other repairs. Then double it, since you are likely to overspend heavily. Some people love engines or electrics but can't do structural bodywork or paint. Be realistic and recognise that it's easy to over-commit, especially if you've a definite schedule in mind for the car to be ready. Good specialist workshops are usually booked up in advance and are not cheap.

Even for those buying an XJ40 for the pleasure of restoration as a hobby, you should choose carefully from the many cars out there in need of repair. The ideal is to buy an abandoned project where somebody has already taken care of the aspects you dislike and left the elements you enjoy most as the ones that need finishing.

Budget for some special tools for both the chassis and power train. For example, the big V12 weighs around 700lb, which is more than many normal engine stands can safely manage.

Beware 'shipwright's disease,' whereby the more parts you refurbish, the more you come across other parts which are now comparatively sub-standard and you decide to replace those also. At least there's a thriving trade in secondhand spares which are very plentiful, and in many cases extremely good value. Some people would even replace the engine or transmission with a reasonable-appearing secondhand one rather than invest time or money in a full rebuild. This is riskier, but for a daily driver non-concours car it is one reasonable option. The cars are not so rare that the whole project cannot be abandoned and a better car sought, with the original serving as a donor for spares, or sold off piecemeal, if necessary.

You need more than a driveway on which to restore these complex cars.

14 Paint problems
– a bad complexion, including dimples, pimples and bubbles

XJ40 cars have large areas of shiny paint, broken up with swage lines and coach lines and trim, to create an overall sleek and balanced effect. Panels are wide and fairly flat compared to other Jaguars so with fewer curves the focus is even more on the quality of the paint itself to give a shiny glossy reflective surface to catch the light. Paint flaws spoil an XJ40 more than lesser cars but are not uncommon. Some of the most vulnerable panels are detachable and accessible from both sides so it ought to be simple enough to ensure a good paint job, but in many cases corners are cut and the car exits the paint shop with superficially good paint that later gives trouble in one of the classic ways described below.

Cracking

Jaguar used various paint types at various times and although the XJ40 was never painted in cellulose (for example) it does not mean that repairs are always done in compatible systems. As well as mismatches, over time many original paints have suffered in extreme climates and for non-original paint all bets are off. Severe cracking is often caused by too heavy an application of paint (or filler beneath). For two-pack modern finishes insufficient stirring of the paint before application can lead to the components being improperly mixed, resulting in cracking. Incompatibility with the paint already on the panel can have a similar effect. Rectification requires stripping entirely or rubbing down to a sound finish before re-spraying.

Poor preparation ruins good paint.

Orange peel

This is as an uneven paint surface looking like a dimpled orange skin, caused by atomized paint droplets not flowing into each other on the painted surface. It's sometimes possible to polish out with paint cutting compound or very fine abrasive paper on a soft block. A re-spray is necessary in severe cases so consult a bodywork repairer/paint shop for advice. If the paint is 2 pack, it will be very hard to flatten. Note that due to production tolerances some XJ40s will not have glass-smooth paint from the factory. This also applies to other modern cars, so the point at which orange peel is classed as a 'problem' is partly subjective.

Overspray and paint reaction.

Crazing

Sometimes the paint takes on a crazed rather than a cracked appearance. This problem can also be caused by a reaction between the underlying surface and the paint. Paint removal and re-spraying the problem area is usually the only solution. Factory paints can craze in desert climates or sometimes even in milder environments, normally worst on horizontal panels.

Paint this crazed is rare.

Blistering

Typically caused by corrosion of the metal beneath the paint. Usually perforation will be found in the metal and the damage will almost always be far worse than suggested by the area of blistering, especially near the wing/sill joins or other vulnerable areas. The metal will have to be repaired before repainting.

Micro blistering

Usually the result of an economy re-spray where inadequate heating or too long in primer coat has allowed moisture to penetrate the primer before top coat spraying. Consult a paint specialist, but usually damaged paint will have to be removed before partial or full re-spraying. Also caused by car covers that don't 'breathe' and encourage moisture absorption.

Fading

Some colours, especially reds, fade under strong sunlight even with polish protection. Sometimes paint restorers or cutting compounds can restore colour but a re-spray may be the only solution if you're unhappy driving a car with serious 'patina'.

Clouding/peeling

Often a problem with metallic paintwork when the clear lacquer becomes UV damaged or peels off. Poorly applied paint may also peel. The remedy is to strip and start again since it is usually not possible merely to reapply lacquer. This is because the base coat will no longer be exactly the right colour and the repair would be noticeable under fresh clearcoat.

Dimples

Dimples or craters in the paintwork are typically caused by residues of polish (particularly silicone) not being removed properly before re-spraying. If present on the original paint (rare) the cause would have been insufficient degreasing at the factory prior to painting. The process was largely automated by this stage, however, so factory paint should be dimple free and any such blemishes point to a respray at some time in the car's life - possibly after accident or vandal damage. Paint removal and repainting is the only solution – localized if possible, extensive if necessary. Remember this problem was caused by insufficient care in the first place.

Lacquer topcoat often peels.

Dents

Small dents are usually easily cured by a 'Dentmaster', or equivalent technician, who can pull or push out the dent (if the paint surface is still intact). Companies offering dent removal services usually come to your home: consult your telephone directory or ask at a local prestige car dealer for personal recommendation. The body shop used by your local dealer to rectify problems with their own stock is usually the best bet for dealing with your car, if top-quality work is your priority. Budget bodywork is usually best left to others.

15 Problems due to lack of use
– just like their owners, XJ40s need exercise!

Given the price of fuel, luxury cars like the XJ40 tend to be kept for weekends and holidays as a 'hobby' purchase, which is a shame. They have always been capable of high mileages and everyday year-round use with good servicing and appropriate anti-corrosion care.

A drive of at least ten miles, once a week, is helpful for the XJ40 but is barely adequate for the bigger engines which are so under-stressed. Try for longer runs and avoid frequently starting the engine and switching off before totally hot, as this is worse than never running the car. The large engines take some warming, and failure to disperse acidic products of combustion will damage even a fine motor. Depending on storage conditions, the interior leather can also benefit from feeding while out of use. Driving also helps disperse rubber compound plasticizers in the tyre carcass to keep it supple.

Seized or sluggish components

The XJ40 has single-piston sliding calipers, front and rear, with the XJ81 (V12) having a different larger front design. Not only the pistons but also the pin sliders can bind during prolonged storage. The best way to maintain brakes is to use them and change the fluid prior to extended lay-up. The Teves ABS system does not need to be exercised to stay healthy, but corrosion and dirt on the wheel sensors or corroded connections at the ABS controller can both become symptomatic after storage.

Fuel can congeal in lines.

The handbrake shoes can bind inside the rear hubs if it is left on in humid conditions that promote rust. Flex hoses to all four calipers can crack with age, although storage does not hasten this.

For manual transmission cars the clutch friction plate may seize to the pressure plate or flywheel from corrosion, so regularly working through the gears and easing the clutch to and fro whilst the engine warms up is a must, if it is not practicable to drive the car because of the season.

Fluids

Old, acidic, engine oil will corrode bearings and machined surfaces, as will

Typical refrigerant leak.

'fresh' oil repeatedly loaded with products of combustion from briefly starting up a large cold engine. Check for a 'mayonnaise' appearance under the filler cap or dipstick. Automatic cars benefit from a change to fresh fluid with fresh corrosion inhibitors before a long lay-up.

Old antifreeze or plain water will ruin both 6 and 12-cylinder water passages and create serious overheating problems if the cooling system is neglected or excessive scale or sealant sludge collects in the radiator. Lack of antifreeze can cause core plugs to be pushed out during winter or crack the block or head, but this is rarer with the V12 which uses an open-deck block with few core plugs. Brake fluid absorbs water from the atmosphere and should be renewed every 2-3 years. Old fluid with high water content causes brake failure if the water promotes rust, and turns to steam vapour near hot braking components. Since all XJ40 models have power steering, this fluid too could be changed before a long lay-up, although the risk of damage is low. Windscreen washer fluid can grow algae and block pipes if plain water is used and left alone for months.

Use fuel stabilizer additives, although opinions differ on whether it is better to fill to the brim to minimise condensation inside the tank, or to almost run the fuel down and stabilise the remainder, prior to adding fresh fuel at the earliest opportunity on recommissioning to dilute any poor fuel.

Tyres

Tyres that take the weight of the car in a single position for long periods develop flat spots. Tyre walls may crack or bulge, so for truly long lay-up leaving the car raised on blocks with the tyres off the ground is good practice. Tyres have approximately a 6-8 year shelf life depending on conditions. Regular use helps preserve tyres by dispersing the plasticizers throughout the compound. Avoid high temperatures and strong sunlight and replace poor tyres on a heavy powerful car like the XJ40. Ask a local tyre specialist how to decipher your tyre's date codes, which vary by country but are usually 4-digit codes with the year and week of manufacture.

Shock absorbers (dampers)

With lack of use, the dampers can corrode on the piston rod. Creaking, groaning, stiff suspension and leaks are signs of this problem. Self-levelling pumps and lines can also corrode and cause malfunction of the system and deterioration of ride quality and car stance.

Rubber and plastic

Radiator hoses can perish and split, possibly resulting in loss of all coolant. The large hose from the pump to the block (under the inlet manifold) is often neglected and deterioration can continue in storage. There are very many hoses for oil, fuel, water, vacuum and brake fluid that can deteriorate from heat, ozone or solvents - or just harden with age. The injectors are clipped to the fuel rail so there is the chance of a seal leak but not hose failure. Do not forget the distributor breathers on V12s and fuel and engine breather hoses. Window and door seals can harden and leak. Steering and suspension gaiters and wiper blades will also harden eventually, especially at high ambient temperatures or outside in strong ultraviolet light. Screen seal materials also harden with age and on standing if in strong sunlight. Dash tops are pretty robust and should not split or crack, although some veneers may suffer varnish clouding or cracking from thermal stress.

Electrics

To keep the battery healthy a trickle charger or battery conditioner will be needed – either on or off the car. Earthing/grounding problems are common when the connections have corroded. Few bullet or spade type electrical connectors are used as standard on XJ40s, having been replaced by modern sealed multi-plugs and sockets. For serious lay-up remove the battery completely. Some microswitches like the transmission interlock and the ones inside door latches can gum up with prolonged lack of use. Other contacts can corrode and cause mystery electrical gremlins on recommissioning.

Exhaust

Exhaust fumes contain water and acids, so even the Ferritic stainless factory exhausts corrode eventually. This can also be from the inside when the car is not used, or is shut off before totally warmed up. The XJ40 has twin exhausts and the surface area is quite large so condensation is an issue if the system is not high-grade stainless. Rubbers can deteriorate and result in poor support of the exhaust by the body. Manifolds and gaskets can cause issues but not due to lay-up. Depending on climate and local wildlife it is possible but rare for vermin or wasps etc to nest inside the exhaust system and choke the engine briefly or for longer when the car is put back into service.

16 The Community
– key people, organisations and companies in the XJ40 world

After a long gestation, the XJ40 was produced for 8 years and saw the company through to the Ford investment, which rapidly paid quality dividends over the life of the model. Though criticised for its square looks (fashionable at the time, but not very 'Jaguar') the XJ40 eventually won people over because it was a much more advanced car than the existing Jaguars and drove superbly. Though they perhaps have never inspired the loyalty of some of the iconic Jaguar models, they did build up a large following, although many were initially bought by businesses. The plentiful supply means an XJ40 is today within reach of almost anyone who wants one.

Plenty of XJ40s are still daily drivers for people to whom they are just an old car, but enough are in the hands of enthusiasts that XJ40s are well-represented in Jaguar club circles. Many specialists exist to serve the market and there are cars in breaker's yards as a ready source of secondhand parts.

There is a dedicated forum to all Series XJ40 models on the internet at www.jag-lovers.org and you can search their archives or ask questions and receive excellent advice on-line.

Clubs

Jaguar Drivers' Club
18 Stuart Street, Luton, Bedfordshire, LU1 2SL
Tel: +44 (0)1582 419332
www.jaguardriver.co.uk
Set up with factory support originally and covering the full range of Jaguars. Has a good web site, excellent magazine and much XJ40 support, insurance schemes and offers valuations etc. Extensive overseas network.

Jaguar Enthusiasts' Club
Abbeywood Office Park, Emma Chris Way
Filton, Bristol, BS34 7JU
Tel: +44 (0)1179 698186
www.jec.org.uk
World's largest Jaguar club, offering the usual good magazine as well as tool hire, specially-commissioned spares and events for every taste. Also very useful JagAds internet and print-based advertisement facility.

Jaguar Clubs of North America
c/o Nelson Rath, 1000 Glenbrook, Anchorage, KY 40223
Tel: +1 502 244 1672
www.jcna.com
Good web site, technical articles and US club network and events calendar. An umbrella organisation for the network of local and regional clubs in the USA.

Jag-Lovers
www.jag-lovers.org
Excellent web-only resource, with great on-line books and discussion forums for

early and late XJ40s and their respective 6- and 12-cylinder engines. Join now and donate a percentage of what it saves you – worth every penny.

The Jaguar Daimler Heritage Trust
Browns Lane, Allesley, Coventry, CV5 9DR
Tel: +44 (0)2476 202141
www.jdht.com
Holders of the official Jaguar archives on production numbers, build configuration and dispatch details, sometimes including first owner information. Sponsored by the Jaguar company in the USA and UK to supply manuals etc and Heritage Certificates confirming the originality of your car's major components.

Jaguar World Monthly
Excellent independent monthly magazine by Kelsey Publishing (www.jaguar-world. com) with regular news and features on the XJ40 and other Jaguars. Many trade advertisements and includes American pages with adverts relevant to the USA.

Parts suppliers
SNG Barratt Group Ltd
UK, USA, Holland, France and Germany addresses
See www.sngbarratt.com
Biggest and best? One of the oldest and most comprehensive spares sources for E-types. Bases in USA/UK/Europe including major remanufacturing capability for electrical parts, sub-assemblies, castings and fabricated parts like bumpers and heater boxes. Much of what is sold by others comes originally from Barratts.

Martin Robey, Pool Road, Camphill Industrial Estate
Nuneaton, CV10 9AE
Tel: +44 (0)1203 386903
www.martinrobey.co.uk
A supplier, along with Jaguar themselves of XJ40 sheet metal, having invested in major press equipment and other production facilities. Also holds large spares stocks for other models.

XKs Unlimited
850 Fiero Lane
San Luis Obispo, CA 93401, USA
Tel 805 544 7864
www.xks.com
Good West Coast supplier with clear line drawings in catalogue and website ordering system.

Terry's Jaguar Parts
117 E. Smith Street
Benton, IL 62812, USA
Tel: 1-800 851 9438
www.terrysjag.com
Mid West specialist with good performance parts range.

Classic Jaguar
9916 Highway 290W
Austin, TX 78736, USA
Tel: 512 288 8800
www.classicjaguar.com
Wide range of parts and upgrades. Runs own web forum.

Useful books
The XJ40 Book
Author: Various contributors. Available as a free download from www.jag-lovers.
org and extremely useful for most systems. Best downloaded complete and then
printed in sections as and when required.

The XJ-S Book
Author: Kirbert Palm and contributors. Another free download from Jag-Lovers and
regarded by many as the definitive collection of all things V12, at least in terms of the
engine itself. Written for the XJ-S rather than the XJ40 but a 'must-read' for learning
about the world's longest-running V12 production engine and includes plentiful
information about the Marelli ignition version and 6.0L as used in the XJ81. In case
you haven't got the message – join Jag-Lovers free now and donate a fraction of
what it saves you to ensure this volunteer site continues to help others.

Jaguar XJ-S, The Essential Buyers Guide
Author: Peter Crespin. A practical and highly-illustrated hands-on guide, to take
you step-by-step through examination and purchase of Jaguar's longest-running
production car of all – the legendary XJ-S Grand Tourer. Covering all engine and
body configurations, this book shows what to look for, what to avoid, and whether
the car is likely to suit your needs, plus relative values and the best places to buy.

Haynes Manuals
Jaguar XJ6 & Sovereign Oct 86-Sept 94 & Service and Repair Manual (#3621)
ISBN 1859602614
Authors: Mike Stubblefield
Hardback: c.200pp
Possibly best general guide apart from factory publications for all 6-cylinder cars.

Jaguar & Daimler 12-cylinder Owners Workshop Manual
ISBN 1850102775
Author: Peter G Strasman
Hardback: 410pp
Good practical guide, not really for the XJ81 but many similarities with the 6.0L
engine used.

6-cylinder XJ40 production (Jaguar, Daimler/VDP combined)

2.9	3.2	3.6	4.0	4.0 LWB	Total
14,148	21,156	83,273	86,175	121	199,672

12-cylinder XJ81 production (Jaguar, Daimler/VDP combined)

6.0	6.0 LWB	Total
3749	50	3799

There are small discrepancies in the above numbers, depending on source. They can be split differently between models and markets but the overall balance of production is as shown.

Technical specifications by model

Specifications changed between years, models and markets, so only an indicative summary is possible here. Please check the appropriate information for specific models/years and markets from other sources, such as original brochures found at www.jag-lovers.org

XJ40 / XJ81 – produced 1986-1994

2.9 (86-90): I6-cylinder 12V SOHC, 2919 cm^3 , 91 x 74.8mm, 165bhp @ 5600rpm & 176lb/ft @ 4000rpm

3.6 (86-90): I6-cylinder 24V DOHC, 3591cm^3, 91 x 93mm, 221bhp @ 5000rpm & 239lb/ft @ 4000rpm

3.2 (90-94): I6-cylinder 24V DOHC, 3239cm^3, 91 x 93mm, 221bhp @ 5250rpm & 220lb/ft @ 4000rpm

4.0 (90-94): I6- cylinder 24V DOHC, 3980cm^3, 91 x 102mm, 223bhp @ 4750rpm & 278lb/ft @ 3650rpm (XJR N/A 248bhp)

6.0 (93-94): V12 cylinder SOHC, 5994cm^3, 90 x 78.5mm, 318bhp @ 5400rpm & 342lb/ft @ 3750rpm

Transmission (manual, 6-cyl): 5-speed Getrag
Transmission (automatic 6-cyl): ZF 4-speed, with electronic mode selection on 4.0L models
Transmission (automatic V12) GM 4L80E electronic 4-speed
Length: 16ft 4.25in (4990mm) width: 6ft 6.75in (2000mm)
Height: 4ft 6.5in (1380mm)
Weight: 3668-3808lb / 1664-1727kg depending on model
Suspension: Fully independent unequal length wishbone at the front, incorporating

anti-dive geometry and mounted on a rubber-isolated subframe with anti-roll bar. Independent rear suspension, with a lower wishbone and upper driveshaft link, using a single coil spring/damper unit per side and hydraulic ride leveling on some models

Brakes: Ventilated power-assisted outboard disc brakes at each corner, with ABS on almost all models

Steering: Power-assisted, with tilt or telescopic column adjustment depending on model. 15in wheels with 16in option on later cars (obligatory 16in on V12)

The Essential Buyer's Guide™

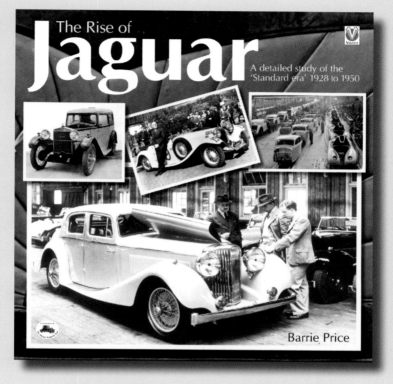

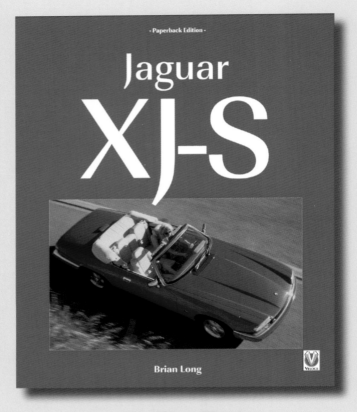

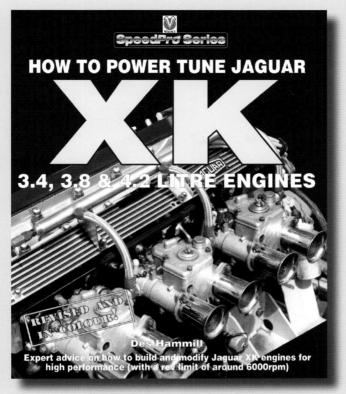

Index

Auctions 40, 41
Automatics 38, 39

Body seals 32
Bodywork 14, 22, 23, 28-30
Bonnet (hood) 23, 29
Books 57
Boot (trunk) 5, 29
Brakes 5, 33, 34

Carpets 36
Certificates 43
Clutch 39
Computer 23, 36, 40
Coolant/cooling 19, 35, 37, 39

Differential 33, 34
Dimensions 5, 59
Distributor 40
Doors 30

Electrics 21, 24, 37, 40
Electronic ignition 19, 40
Engine 20, 21, 24, 38
Exhaust system 32, 33
Extras 47, 48

Floors 29, 30
Fuel consumption 6
Fuel lines 30
Fuel tank 30
Fuses 36

Gauges 36
Gearbox 38, 39
Glass 33

Handbrake 5, 34
Headlamps 31
Headliner 25, 35
Hood (bonnet) 23, 29
Hoses 37

Ignition 19. 40
Inspection 17, 19, 20
Instruments 36
Insurance 7
Interior trim 22, 26, 35, 36

Legal issues 16
Limited slip differential 21, 34
Luggage space 5, 6

Model types 12, 13

Oil leaks 39, 40
Oil pressure 39

Paint problems 49-51
Panel fit 22, 28
Paperwork 42, 43
Parts suppliers 56,57
Power steering 34, 35, 40
Production numbers 58

Radiator 37
Registration documents 16, 43
Restoration 47, 48

Seats 5, 6
Service history 43
Servicing 8, 9
Shock absorbers 33, 34
Sills 29
Specialists 56, 57
Specifications 58, 59
Steering 40
Suspension 20, 21, 33 - 35

Transmission 38, 39
Tyres 32

Underside 23, 29

Valuation 12, 13, 43
Vehicle checks 17, 19, 20
Viewing 14, 15
VIN number 16

Water pump 37
Web sites 55, 56
Weights 59
Wheels 32
Windscreen 33
Wipers 33